By Neil Postman and Charles Weingartner

THE SOFT REVOLUTION

TEACHING AS A SUBVERSIVE ACTIVITY

LINGUISTICS:
A Revolution in Teaching

the Soft Revolution

by Neil Postman
AND
Charles Weingartner

A STUDENT HANDBOOK
FOR TURNING SCHOOLS AROUND

DELACORTE PRESS
NEW YORK

Grateful acknowledgment is given to the following for permission
to reprint excerpts from copyrighted material:

"Parent Power" from *Culture and Commitment* by Margaret Mead. Copyright © 1970 by Margaret Mead. Reprinted by permission of Doubleday & Company, Inc. and The Bodley Head.

An Alternative Future For America by Robert Theobald. Copyright © 1968 by Robert Theobald. Reprinted by permission of The Swallow Press, Chicago.

"1066 And All That" from *Historians' Fallacies* by David Hackett Fischer. Used by permission of Harper & Row, Publishers.

Cartoon "Grin And Bear It" by Lichty. © Copyright Field Enterprises, Inc. 1970. Courtesy of Publishers Hall, Syndicate.

Cartoon "Love It! Save It!" by Bill Mauldin. Copyright © 1970 The Chicago Sun-Times. Reproduced by courtesy of Wil-Jo Associates, Inc. and Bill Mauldin.

Cartoon "No! Please . . . I'm relevant . . ." by Ed Fisher. Copyright © 1969 Saturday Review, Inc. Used by permission of the publisher and the author.

And our thanks to Cynthia Lowery for permission to use her 1970 Christmas card, "Power to the Peaceful."

HOW TO TELL IF THIS BOOK IS FOR YOU

This book was written mainly for students, somewhere between the ages of fifteen and twenty-five. But not all of them. We are not talking to those who have been able to accommodate themselves, without discomfort, to the schooling process. Neither are we talking to those whose discomfort is so acute that they are prepared to burn buildings down. It doesn't take much intelligence to do either; and, in any case, our own temperament and knowledge severely limit what we are able to say to such students. We have the impression that somewhere between accommodation and hysteria there are millions of students who:

are dissatisfied with the ways in which their education is conducted,
are searching for effective ways to change the situation, and
do not feel that all the avenues for non-violent change have been exhausted.

SO,

IF you think you are doing all right and that the present educational system will help to facilitate your survival;
IF you think that our present leaders (educational and otherwise) have a competent and benign vision of the future;
IF you think that radical change in education is unnecessary;
IF you lack the interest and energy to serve as an agent of change

this book was not written for you.

ON THE OTHER HAND,

IF you enjoy insulting people and keeping them in a condition of outrage;

IF you think the world is divided into good guys and bad guys and you're a good guy,

IF you think that everything is so confused, or complex, or controlled, that nothing can really be done to change things, or

IF you think that *everything* must be changed before *anything* can, you may be right . . .

but this is not your book either.

If you are not a student, don't stop reading—for awhile, anyway. If you are a teacher, or a parent, or school administrator, or politician, or just a romantic who still believes in the improvability of social institutions, you may find it useful to know what advice we are offering. But the point is that this book was not written for you and therefore contains no statements *intended* to please you, mobilize you, or, for that matter, irritate you. You are welcome, but you are not the guest.

Of course, even if the guest list is restricted to students, the party turns out to be a pretty big one nonetheless, and puts together people of very diverse character. If you are fifteen years old, you are probably a sophomore in high school, and may think you don't have much in common with a twenty-five-year-old graduate student (who may also be a teacher). We concede that there are important differences, and where our handbook has something to say to a high school student that is not relevant to a college student, or vice versa, it will be apparent enough. But our book was conceived on the assumption that most students have more in common than they have been led to believe; that, in fact, the "student revolt" cuts across grade levels, geographical regions, ethnic backgrounds, and age groups.

Hanging on an office wall at New York University is a message sent to us by a third-grader from Palo Alto. It reads: "School is Shit." Members of the Montgomery County Student Alliance (mostly high school students) have produced a document called *Wanted: A Humane Education*. Its main conclusions are that school is based on fear, that it compels students to be dishonest, that it destroys the "natural" joy of learning, and that it promotes obedience to authority. In Jerry Farber's underground pamphlet, "The Student As Nigger," he talks of the role of college students: "The faculty tell him what courses to take . . . ; they tell him what to read, what to write, and, frequently, where to set the margins on his typewriter. They tell him what is true and what isn't. Some teachers insist that they encourage dissent but they're almost always jiving and every student knows it. Tell the man what he wants to hear or he'll fail your ass out of the course." A study sponsored by the American Political Science Association concluded that graduate students are working under a climate of "threat and fear" of failure. Apparently, there are very few students who escape, no matter where they are. Everywhere the complaints are the same: not enough freedom, not enough responsibility, not enough relevance, not enough love, too much bureaucracy, too much labeling, and too much fear. But here's the main point. We are not going to argue the case against the present arrangements for education. We've already done a book on that (and so have many others). If you do not know what are the main lines of the indictment, this handbook won't make much sense to you. As we said, this book is for those who do know, who want to consider alternatives, and who want to know how to achieve them, without contributing to the destruction of their society or themselves. If you're anywhere near that, these pages were written for your use.

Here's what you will find in them: **advice, maxims, homilies, metaphors, models, case studies, rules, commentaries, jokes, sayings, and a variety of other things** you may be able to use right now or in the years ahead to hasten educational change. Think of our handbook as you would a cookbook: there's a recipe for stew and a recipe for Quiche Lorraine, but you don't have to make a stew *before* you make the quiche. You choose or put together the recipe you need for your situation. In other words, our manner of presentation is not sequential. We do not wish to give the impression that there exists some lineal approach to change—as if you could begin at point A and move to point Z. You begin where you can with what you've got (including your own appetite), and you move up, down, around, and forward, depending on what is possible for you at a given time and in a given place.

As long as there is movement, and you feel it is toward freedom, creativity, and responsibility, you're probably doing the right thing. And if our handbook helps you, *we've* done the right thing. Probably.

WHAT'S A
Soft Revolution?

As of this writing, Donald St. George Reeves is eighteen years old, black, and a senior at the High School of Music and Art in New York. He and five other students formed a group called The Student Rights Coalition. Its purpose is to press for adoption of a "negotiated bill of student rights." Reeves is chairman. He and the others have recruited about five thousand members, mostly from schools with serious problems. Reeves wants to make student government something other than "a big joke." Commenting on his success at organizing, Reeves was quoted as saying, "It's surprising how much you can get away with by wearing a jacket and a tie."

Marc Stanton is twenty-one, and a junior at NYU. He and thirty-five undergraduates have been helping ghetto kids who are having trouble in school. They "tutor" them for an hour or so on a Saturday or Sunday. Then spend the rest of the day visiting museums and parks. "Most of us feel obligated to help," says Stanton. "This is something we can do instead of just talking. The results are quite evident. We walk down the street and we get mobbed by kids."

In Cheltenham, England, five kids—John Stemp, eleven; Ruper Wilson, seven; Joanna Wilson, eight; Frank Moran, ten; and Julie Harper, nine—formed an anti-crime squad which they called The Secret Five. Within three days after they started, they had solved their first crime. Joanna spotted a teenager who was circling around on a bicycle and apparently signaling to

[1]

someone in a house. She alerted two other members of The Secret Five, and they observed two youths carrying goods from the house to an automobile. The Secret Five wrote a report, presented it to the police, and the thieves were eventually arrested. The Secret Five titled its report "The Story of the Strange Man."

Robert Marks was twenty-eight years old when he was "invited" not to return the following year to the school where he had been teaching. Apparently Marks wasn't sufficiently interested in grading, tests, and the standard curriculum. Also, he and his students talked a great deal about "unauthorized" subjects. Marks didn't quite know what to do when he was let go. So he started his own school, which is now called The New Prospect Day School. In Marks' school, the teachers don't give grades or tests, and everyone talks all the time about "unauthorized" subjects.

Five years after the assassination of Malcolm X, about two hundred people gathered at his grave to honor him on the anniversary of his birth. There were several angry speeches made, some of them urging violence. But Malcolm's sister, Mrs. Ella Collins, apparently wasn't impressed. "Don't let him down," she scolded the audience. "Stop sleeping all day. Learn to develop your mind and learn to do something positive for a change. For me, for him, but most of all for you. Stop playing the role of children." Most of the audience was young. Some were white.

"Let me suggest to you that we live on a vast plain on which there are a large number of castles. These castles, representing our institutions, are unguarded: The moats are empty and the drawbridges are down. All we have to do is walk into the castles —the old institutions—and take everything out of them that would be valuable for the future. It is necessary to tiptoe in because there are some people who will get mad if you disturb them. So you move quietly. Unfortunately, the people who have been trying to get change up to now haven't been satisfied to tiptoe in and take what they wanted. They have done it in a different way. They assembled outside the castle and they blew their trumpets and claimed they were coming in to take over. The defenders, in a last access of energy, felt challenged to try to defend the castle. Normally, young and vigorous people who want to get change would win the battle, but actually they don't because the castles have installed atomic weapons and the attackers get wiped out." (Robert Theobald, *An Alternative Future for America.* Chicago: Swallow Press, 1968.)

John Calatayud is a teenager who goes to Jamaica High School in New York. He teaches astronomy to elementary school children who belong to an extracurricular group called The Star Gazers. "I'm a pretty good teacher," he says. Why? "Because I can still remember what it's like *not* to know astronomy. So I always know how to explain what the kids don't know."

Bill Ahlhauser, Belinda Behne, Jim Boulet, and about thirty other teenagers, most of them "successful" students, got fed up with the standard brand schooling given them in Milwaukee. So they stopped going, and started their own school. Their school is based on the assumptions that all students have serious personal interests and that these interests should be the starting point for education. The assistant superintendent for Pupil Personnel, Theodore Kuemmerlein, is required to enforce compulsory attendance in Milwaukee, but he says he doesn't quite know how to deal with this situation. The courts will have to rule on how legal the new school is. Kuemmerlein adds: "Anytime your top students leave school, it concerns you. It makes you wonder what we're not offering to meet their needs."

Each of these "cases" reflects an attitude or an action that is a small part of the process we call a "soft revolution." The soft revolution has as its purpose the renewal and reconstruction of educational institutions without the use of violence. Violence changes the subject. It is counter-productive. It is plain dumb, at best. At worst, it damages and destroys human beings, and we just don't need any more of that.

The soft revolution is characterized by a minimum of rhetoric, dogma, and charismatic leadership. It consists of a point of view (and concomitant strategies) that is serious, but not solemn. Solemnity seems to be a strategy invented to make something that's basically ridiculous seem important. Among the purposes of the soft revolution is to make visible the ridiculousness of our solemn tribal beliefs and rituals—and *that* requires a sense of humor.

The central purpose of the soft revolution is to help all of us get it all together in the interests of our *mutual* survival. It may try to reform an existing system or start a better one from scratch. It all depends on what one is prepared to do and what is possible. Its objective is to make changes in the way things are being done. Profound changes, where possible—and where that is not possible, simple improvements. It begins anywhere and anytime someone finds room enough to do something that is better than what's going on. When enough things have been done, you may find that a new system has happened. Some people do not like this idea because it represents "piecemeal reform." They are wrong. When piecemeal reform is inadequate, the reason is that not enough pieces have yet been reformed. Besides, to quote Mr. Theobald again, "There is no possibility of a revolution if one means by this that one can change totally a set of cultural attitudes. It can't be done."

When you are making a soft revolution, you need not concern yourself with every problem in the universe. Only one or two. The easiest way to dissipate the desire for a particular change is to convince yourself that the change does not get at the general problem. Bureaucrats know this perfectly well, which is why they prefer to deal with those who think cosmic rather than with those who think specific.

When you are making a soft revolution, you are not required to assume that you are absolutely right; nor that you are, in all respects, more virtuous than those whose ideas you would like to "disappear." All that is required is your considered judgment that you may have a better idea.

When you are making a soft revolution, you do not always need a large organization. Sometimes, five people doing the right thing the right way can do the job. This implies that individual effort can make a difference, even if only to twenty people. Beware of the man who passes up that opportunity because he is not satisfied with helping so few. He probably works for the CIA. Beware also of those who devote themselves entirely to revolution. They are usually very boring, and find it impossible to retain a sense of humor. They are one-dimensional people. If a man becomes obsessed with an idea, he probably loves his obsession more than his idea.

The soft revolution regards *anything* that makes any one, some, or all of us damaged or dead as plain-assed dumb. If you kill yourself or someone else in a misbegotten attempt to survive, you have obviously done a dumb thing, and the soft revolution is simply against dumb things. If schools weren't doing dumb things we wouldn't need a soft revolution in the first place.

When you are making a soft revolution, you are free to change your mind—and yourself in the process. In fact, by using this option, you can learn how and why other people change *their* minds, and you will, as a consequence, be a better soft revolutionary.

The basic metaphor of a soft revolution is judo. As the term suggests, its primary use is in the defense of self against system. When you are using judo, you do not oppose the strength of your adversary. You use your adversary's strength against himself, and in spite of himself (in fact, *because* of himself). You do not need judo when your own strength is greater than your adversary's. In that case you can, if you wish, smash him to bits. But that is clearly not the situation in relation to change in education. The bureaucracies that govern educational institutions, while not as powerful as certain others in our society, still have the forces of precedent, law, academic prejudice, economic coercion, tradition, and inertia behind them. And when those fail, there are city governments and state legislatures. And when those, too, fail— the police or national guard. The confrontation tactics of student militants during the past five years have not been without result. But considering the energy that has been spent, the effort has been impressively inefficient. The SYSTEM remains not only intact but *better than ever prepared to deal with confrontations.* The schools are still murdering almost everybody, intellectually and spiritually, and in spite of all the highpitched noises, there is no decent "game plan" to stop them.

Judo is the game plan. With it, you do not "work within the system"—any more than you run head-on into it. You use the system against itself to work for needed change. But to use the principles of judo to facilitate educational change, one must

understand exceedingly well the structure of the system one is dealing with,
understand the symbology of that system,
understand the psychology of those who comprise the system.

This requires rather more thought and self-discipline than spitting in a cop's face.

The *hard* revolution is counter-productive because it provokes violence, reaction, recrimination, retaliation, loss of strategic support and, all in all, produces more problems than it solves. It also requires no brains or wit at all. Any fool with long hair can stand on a corner and scream "Pigs!" or "Do it!" or "Power to the People!" It's not only fatal, it's no fun.

Power to the
Peaceful

JUDO

When you are using judo as a metaphor for effecting change, you must have a realistic grasp of how things stand. For instance, here are some facts that will not change in the near future. They are "obvious," which means many people act as if they do not know about them.

1. People who have functioned successfully within a system are generally unwilling to have the system change, much less work to change it.
2. They are not "evil" (at least, no more than you). They just don't want to let go of a good thing.
3. No one (including you) wants to change *all* his beliefs. In fact, it is probably impossible to do so and retain your sanity.
4. That is why people sometimes prefer problems that are familiar to solutions that are not.
5. People tend to react to their symbols as if the symbols were the things they represent. (This may be the most critical fact for anyone wanting change to remember and act on.)
6. People are actually *afraid* of many words. (You too.)
7. Very often, people do not see a connection between the way they live their lives and their ideas, which may be just as well. In other words, there are a great many "good" people with bad opinions and "bad" people with good ones. Distinguishing between the two is a helluva job, but usually worth it.
8. It is not true, as some humanists like to say, that there is a shortage of moral outrage. There is plenty around for everyone. But moral outrage, by itself, does not bring needed change.

Here is an example of the application of these eight observations in a specific and actual situation where judo was used. The setting is a meeting of the citizens of a community not far from New York City. About three hundred people are present, almost all of them parents of students in junior and senior high school. The subject to be discussed is a proposal for a radical experiment in education. This is the proposal, as it was put into the hands of members of the audience:

Most school programs assume (1) that knowledge is best presented and comprehended when organized into "subjects," (2) that most subjects have a specific "content," (3) that the content of these subjects is more or less stable, (4) that a major function of the teacher is to "transmit" this content, (5) that the most practical place to do this is in a room within a centrally·located building, (6) that students learn best in 45-minute periods which meet five times a week, (7) that students are learning when they are listening to their teacher, reading their texts, doing their assignments, and otherwise "paying attention" to the content being transmitted, and, finally, (8) that all of this must go on as preparation for life.

The program we wish you to consider disputes these assumptions and offers, instead, the following ones: (1) that learning takes place best, *not* when it is conceived as a preparation for life, but when it occurs in the context of real daily life, (2) that each learner, ultimately, must organize his own learning in his own way, (3) that "problems" and personal interests are a more realistic structure than are "subjects" for organizing learning experiences, (4) that students are capable of directly and authentically participating in the intellectual and social life of their community, and (5) that the community badly needs them to do this.

This program hopes to employ the curiosity, energy, and idealism of youth in a context which permits both the students and the community to change. Thus, the program reduces the reliance on classrooms and school buildings, and transforms the relevant problems of the community into the students' "curriculum."

Here's how it would work: This community, like so many others, has serious problems with traffic control, crime and law enforcement, strikes, race relations, urban blight, drug addiction, garbage disposal, air pollution, and medical care. Students would be formed into teams, each team consisting of a teacher, a high school senior, perhaps a lay member of the community, and ten or twelve students. Their task would be to select one of these problems for study, with a view toward inventing authentic, practical solutions to it. They would *do* whatever they needed to do in order to learn about the problem and to communicate to others their own solutions. These *doings* would amount to their curriculum. For example, imagine that one team has selected the "crime problem" for study. Some students would spend two or three weeks at the police station, serving in some capacity that would allow them to observe the problem from the perspective of the police. (Some might even go out on calls with police officers.) Others might meet regularly at the criminal court, observing the problem from that vantage point. Students could go on interviewing assignments, talking to people who are ostensibly knowledgeable about the problem: insurance men, police officers from other towns, ex-convicts, prison wardens, merchants, judges, and town officials. Students could review the available literature (both nonfiction and fiction), correspond with prisoners, and write to law enforcement officers in other places. The classroom would be used as a place of assembly when students need to assess their findings and to plan and organize additional inquiries. But most of the students' "school life" would be spent *outside* the school, where the realities of the problems being studied are to be found. Included in the whole process must be a serious attempt to offer solutions and to communicate these to the appropriate people. This might require meeting in school for the purpose of writing resolutions, letters, pamphlets, handbills, and reports. Or the students might wish to publish a newsletter about the problem, or produce an audio tape for broadcasting on the local radio station, or produce a film for presentation to the community. The possibilities are almost inexhaustible.

Much of the teacher's work would involve making arrangements for the students' daily and weekly activities—for example, arranging with the police, or the courts, or the radio station, or the newspaper, for the most beneficial "internship" experience and the most useful outlets from which the students could reach the community. The nature and locale of the students' activities would depend on the problem they are studying. A study of medical care problems would lead students to hospitals, doctors' offices, homes for the aged, the local public health agency, welfare agencies, and so on. A study of race relations might lead them to the Chamber of Commerce, the courts, the newspaper office, churches, and the like.

One group of students, when asked what problem they would be interested in looking into—if such a program were implemented —chose, understandably, the selective service process in their town. Here are some of the questions they formulated:

1. Who is on the draft board?
2. How is one selected to serve on the board?
3. What are the political and social philosophies of the men presently on the board?
4. How much discretion do they have in classifying men?
5. On what bases do they make their decisions?
6. To what or whom are they responsible?

Naturally, the answers to these questions cannot be found in a classroom. One has to go to libraries, newspaper morgues, government agencies, people's offices and homes, the draft board itself—just about anyplace but school.

Students might also meet on a regular basis in seminars with adults to consider community problems. These seminars would be held in public buildings and private homes, and would offer opportunities for exchanges of views on matters of common interest, and the undertaking of joint student-adult projects. For instance, a seminar could be held on the selective service problem, in which members of the draft board could meet with students to exchange information, points of view, fears, even hostilities.

Another aspect of this new "curriculum" would offer students the opportunity to pursue special interests independently or with the guidance of adults (not necessarily teachers). Students might paint in an artist's studio, write poems and stories, build a TV set, tutor younger students, do scientific research in a laboratory, act in a play, serve as apprentices to the manager of a local bank or to the partners in a local law firm. All of these activities would bring students into regular contact with adults and, hopefully, generate among both groups respect for differences of opinion.

In brief, the major idea of this proposal is that the community itself would become a laboratory for the interests and inquiries of students. The classroom would be only one of the many resources that the students might choose to use. For certain purposes, it might be used in more or less conventional ways (e.g., for the study of a foreign language or for instruction in typing). For other purposes, it might be used for small-group workshops in which the progress and problems of student inquiries could be analyzed. But the major source of the students' learning experiences would be the community, not the classroom.

Now, without support from the community, the chances of implementing such a proposal as this would be nil. On first acquaintance, the idea is simply too "radical" for most taxpayers, and is certainly fraught with peril for school administrators. The proponents of the proposal, therefore, have called a public meeting to try to draw a favorable response from as many taxpayers as possible. The audience, of course, is possessed of the usual number of prejudices, including a fear of change. The speaker who will present the proposal has been warned that the audience is not entirely displeased with the existing arrangements for education, and that they are especially nervous about any innovations in education which might cost them more money. (Fact #9: Most people do not like to spend money unless it will produce some immediate gratification.)

Many of the people in the audience were "successful" students in school, and find it hard to understand why a kid would be unable to "take advantage of the existing opportunities offered him." At the same time, they know that the situation in the school is dreadful, especially for blacks and lower-class whites. (Fact #10: It is not uncommon for people to believe in two contradictory ideas simultaneously.) The dropout rate in the school system is high; there is tension between black and white students, and conflict between teachers and almost all students. There have already been two "riots," both in the school cafeteria. The presence of a police car in front of the school is now routine.

With this information about his audience—their expectations, interests, concerns, doubts, and fears—firmly in mind, the chief proponent of the proposal chooses to use a judo approach to gain acceptance of the idea. Here are the major points he makes in his remarks to the audience:

> A major characteristic of the American culture is that it is pluralistic. If pluralism means anything, it means the availability of options. Where there are no real options, you have a fraudulent pluralism—the name without the reality. This is true in business, as well as in government. It is also true in education.
>
> At present, our educational system is monolithic. One has no choice but to accept the sole approach to learning offered by the

schools. The situation if not un-American, is not American in spirit.

Imagine a supermarket which offers only one brand of food; a political system which offers only one candidate; an economic system which offers only one choice of occupation. Imagine a school system which offers only one set of assumptions about learning.

What this proposal does is to make available *to those who want it* another approach to learning. No one would be forced into the program. Only those students who wish to join, and who have their parents' permission to do so, would be accepted.

The program would be an "experiment." If it does not work out, it will be stopped. If it does, perhaps this school system can eventually offer a third or even a fourth approach to learning.

The audience did not, of course, rise as one to offer its applause and unqualified support. But it *liked* what it heard. The speech did not require the audience to change all of its views, only one. It did not require the audience to repudiate its past experience. It did not contain frightening words, and, in fact, contained words that the audience is accustomed to hearing and enjoys hearing. The speaker did not claim to be superior to his audience. He did not propose to scrap a system in which the audience has an emotional and intellectual stake, but merely to extend it. In fact, to extend it for reasons that most of the audience approves. Moreover, although the speaker is as devoted to educational change as anyone could be, there was nothing in his remarks which he does not believe. It is true, though, that he *omitted* from his speech certain beliefs which the audience would reject. These include his opposition to the Vietnam War, his opposition to racism in any form, his opposition to the FBI, the CIA, the ABM, the SST, MIRV, and various other threats to America. He omitted expressing these beliefs because they were not relevant to *the achievement of the particular change he favors.* This may be called good public relations—which means having a good relationship with a public. Since establishing a good relationship with this particular public was essential to effecting change, the speaker tried to do just that. He was successful. As of this writing, the program is in operation in that community. That's judo. That's a soft revolution.

"You Mean, It Isn't?"

Some years ago, a successful American businessman had a serious identity crisis. He sought help from psychiatrists, but nothing came of it, for there were none who could tell him the meaning of life—which is what he wanted to know. By and by, he learned of a venerable and incredibly wise guru who lived in a mysterious and most inaccessible region of the Himalayas. Only *that* guru, he came to believe, could tell him what life means and what his role in it ought to be. So he sold all his worldly possessions and began his search for the all-knowing guru. He spent eight years wandering from village to village throughout the Himalayas in an effort to find him. And then one day he chanced upon a shepherd who told him where the guru lived and how to reach the place. It took him almost a year to find it, but he eventually did. There he came upon his guru, who was indeed venerable—in fact, well over one hundred years old. The guru consented to help the man, especially when he learned of all the sacrifices the man had made toward this end.

"What can I do for you, my son?" asked the guru.

"I need to know the meaning of life," said the man.

To this, the guru replied without hesitation. "Life," he said, "is a river without end."

"A river without end?" said the man, in startled surprise. "After coming all this way to find you, all you have to tell me is that life is a river without end?"

"You mean, it isn't?" asked the guru.

An old joke. But with a point worth noting. Gurus aren't the only people who are not quite sure of what they're doing. And here's a big, badly concealed secret: there is probably no professional group more unsure of itself than teachers. Considering the state of the art, this is hardly surprising. Almost all education conferences are characterized by self-doubting, and sometimes even self-mutilation. Ask a teacher, in a soft way, why he thinks some procedure he uses is good for students, and he will reply, "You mean, it isn't?" Ask in a hard way, and you get something different. Then, he will react the way most people do when they are unsure of themselves: He will rededicate himself to the behavior you challenged.

Because their assumptions are so precariously held, teachers are more susceptible to change than almost any other group—provided that you follow these rules:

1. Do not tell a teacher flatly that he's wrong. (It really scares the hell out of him. And out of lawyers, ministers, writers, and almost everyone else except brain surgeons. Besides, you can't really be sure that he *is* wrong.)

2. When you think he is wrong, suggest an alternative procedure. (Whenever you point out a school problem to someone, whether he's a teacher, an administrator, a parent, or a community representative, ALWAYS have alternative *solutions* to suggest, in some order of priority, as soon as you've laid the problem on him.

One of the reasons for doing this is that most poeple who have responsibility for schools are already up to their armpits in problems, and the last thing they need is having another one to deal with. Chances are that even if they're sympathetic, they might not come up with a solution that would seem to you to be responsive to the problem.

SO, if you have some possible solutions, and the more feasible they are, the better, the odds are that *your* solutions will be given a try simply because no one else has the time, the energy, or the inclination to figure out anything better.

Another reason for doing this is that philosophically, most teachers are committed to the idea that there is no single, royal road to truth. In practice, many of them act as if there were, but in theory they are irresistibly drawn to pluralism. The idea is for you to help them get their theory and practice together.)

3. In suggesting alternatives, try to use language that is familiar to the teacher and that he likes to hear. (Like *evaluation,*

experiment, progress, inquiry, initiative, motivation. This is an essential part of the judo method of effecting change.)

4. No teacher will refuse a student's request for help. Therefore, whenever possible, make it appear that your alternative is intended to help *you* learn, not your teacher.

5. Your suggestion must not in any way increase the paperwork that the teacher must do. (If there is one thing that teachers *are* sure of, it is that they hate paperwork, and for good reason: like you they have better things to do.)

6. If at all possible, in supporting your alternative, make reference to the *Encyclopedia of Educational Research.* (You can make up any study you want, since not one teacher in a hundred has even heard of the *Encyclopedia,* and not one in a thousand has ever looked at it. Frankly, this is to their credit since there is very little of value in it. And yet, teachers have a reverence—a fear perhaps—and, therefore, a weakness for the citation of educational research.)

7. Do not go over the teacher's head, until you have tried everything else. (In judo, as in other adversary encounters, you don't "play dirty" unless forced into it.)

Here's how this would all work: Imagine you are a high school student who, along with five or six others, are being squeezed dry by English grammar. Your teacher appears to be committed to the "subject" and relentlessly keeps it up. The first thing you must understand is that your teacher does not know whether or not grammar is really good for you. He is doing this because (1) it was done to him when he was a student, (2) he probably can't think of too many other things to do in its place, (3) it is prescribed in the syllabus, and (4) it is a "subject" which is relatively easy to give a test on. You also know, because you are reading this book, that you must not tell him you know all these things. Instead, you tell him that you understand that his reason for teaching grammar is to help improve the writing and speaking of students. He will probably agree to this. Suspiciously. You then propose an educational experiment along the following lines: Half of the students in the class will substitute an extensive reading program for their grammar lessons. At the end of the term, the writing of students in the experimental group will be evaluated in the same way as the writing of those in the control group. ("Control group" is a valuable phrase. It will reveal at once that your group is not a bunch of dingalings.) Your hypotheses (another great word) are that (1) grammar study does not help to improve writing, (2) it may actually hinder the improvement of writing, and (3) extensive reading may be the answer. You also point out that studies reported in the *Encyclopedia of Educational Research* suggest that much research is needed in this area. In addition, you mention that independent readers probably ought to be used to evaluate the papers. (You thereby relieve the teacher of an odious task—reading papers.)

If your teacher agrees to your proposal, here is what you will accomplish: (1) you will free yourself from the boring grammar lessons; (2) if you actually do the reading, you might enjoy yourself; (3) if you don't do the reading, it won't make any difference, since grammar does not help anyone to write better; (4) all your hypotheses may be right—especially number 2—in which case you'll be a better writer; (5) you will probably be regarded by your teacher as a serious student. This last is important because it sets the stage for more "experiments."

One such reform as this would not make a great deal of difference, but imagine what a difference it would make if just fifty students in a high school initiated experiments in ten different subjects. You would have reformed the curriculum of that high school.

Of course, it is entirely possible that your teacher will *not* agree to the proposal. He may get the impression that you and your classmates are using the old put-on. In a way, you are. So the situation will call for a considerable degree of artistry and seriousness. We assume that you understand the process we are describing is not something done simply for kicks, but is a tactic that, in turn, is part of a larger strategy. We also assume you understand that the example was chosen to show, in the most uncomplicated way, how to turn to your own advantage certain facts about your teachers. Most of the problems you will need to solve are more complex than this. But if you can pull this off, you will have passed your JUNIOR SOFT REVOLUTIONARY TEST.

An Open Letter to a Faculty Member from One of His Revolutionary Students

(SOFT VARIETY)

Dear Professor _____,

I know how worried you are about the survival of our college. It may seem strange to you to be told that I am just as worried, but I am. Somehow, everyone's got the impression that I and other "revolutionary" students are the cause of the threat. But we are only its symptoms. The threat comes from the incredible changes going on around us, and what we are trying to say is that unless this fact is given immediate and profound attention by educators, they will soon find themselves out of influence, out of students, and out of work. I am writing to you about this because I think you know what I am talking about. I don't propose, therefore, to bore you with exhortations or scare you with threats. What I would like to do is explain why I think we are having so much trouble, and suggest some ways of correcting the situation. I am doing this in a letter because in this form I can express my thoughts quietly, and you can read them quietly. There's always a lot of noise at the barricades.

I want to begin by mentioning something I heard you say once in class: One must never confuse the outward forms of existence with inner life. I think this distinction is crucial in understanding our situation. There are at present dozens of institutions whose outward forms remain intact, but whose purposes have long ago ceased to be viable. I think, for instance, that the Vietnam War is an excellent example of this. The fighting goes on. The men and materials are moved around. The kill ratio is favorable. The medals are awarded. The death notices are properly sent. All the forms of military activity are preserved, but the point of it all has been completely lost. What is the purpose of the war? No one seems to know any more, even those who once told us they did. The President regards it as a liability. The mass media are bored with it. The middle class tries not to think about it. Even my contemporaries seem past outrage. In short, the Vietnam War is over, and has been for several years; and yet it goes on because no one seems to know quite how to stop it. That is the way of things with institutions. Their forms, including their rhetoric, always survive their functions. This is the case with our political system, with our religious institutions, with our marriages, with our cities. It is certainly the case with most of our schools.

When was the last time you really looked at what goes on in a junior or senior high school, for instance? Outwardly, the school looks like it always has, except that more windows are broken now. The students are there; the teachers are there; the cafeteria and gym are

there; the textbooks are there. There are
homework assignments written on the blackboard.
But once you get beyond all that, you find
that the school has become something entirely
different from what it was intended to be. Some
say the school has become quite like a prison.
It is certainly more a house of detention than
attention. The teachers have lost any real hope
of teaching; the students do not expect to do
any real learning; the administrators are
not serious about anything like "curriculum
reform." The inner life of these schools has
not survived. There is the smell of death in
every room. And one can begin to sense the same
smell even on college campuses located in the
most bucolic settings.

The most vivid metaphor I know for what I
am trying to say here are those old TV commercials for Salem cigarettes, which tell us that
you can take Salem out of the country, but you
can't take the country out of Salem. But we all
know it's not the country that you can't get
out of Salem. It's the lung cancer. And no
amount of advertising flack will fix that. It
may well be that "curriculum reform" is the
equivalent of adding a charcoal filter to a
cigarette: It creates the illusion of promoting
life while doing just the opposite. And so,
what I want to do in this letter is to identify
what I believe to be the most toxic and even
lethal assumption upon which most colleges are
based. When that's done, I want to suggest to
you some alternative ways of organizing a college—all of which become possible when one
rejects this central assumption.

Stated simply, that assumption is that
adults are smarter than kids—from which it
follows that professors are smarter than students. However defensible this assumption may

have been in the past, in my opinion the evidence is clear that it is false today. For instance, one meaning of "smarter" might be that professors are better at identifying and solving relevant problems than students. Well, then, who were the first to see that our colleges were in trouble, and who made the first attempts to do something about it? Whose idea was it to have black studies programs and interdisciplinary approaches? Whose idea was it to debureaucratize the colleges? Whose idea was it to demilitarize American universities? Whose idea was it to offer substantial opposition to the war in Vietnam? Whose idea was it to call attention to environmental pollution? Whose idea was it to try to organize and defeat the institutionalized oppression of black people? Whose idea was it to initiate a movement to oppose oppression of women? Well, it was not our professors', and although my generation has not always been effective or even sensible in solving these problems, they have employed such power as they have or can generate toward that end. And that fact, all by itself, disputes the claim of the professorial class to intellectual and moral superiority over their students.

Another meaning of "smarter" is that professors have more knowledge of "subjects" than students. That is probably true, if you mean by subjects those that were found in college catalogues twenty-five years ago and which still take up the most space in catalogues today. But if you began to add courses at our college in cinematography, ecology, photography, electronics, narcotics, urban affairs, race relations, birth control, mass media, and popular culture, to name just a few, you would quickly find out who were the legitimate teachers and

who the legitimate students. At present, the
only way professors can maintain their status
as clearly more knowledgeable than their students is to insist that the subjects they know
about are fundamental, and the subjects we know
about or are interested in are derivative or
trivial. This is, of course, a semantic trick
which is already being exposed but, in any
case, will lose all its dazzle within the next
five years. Even further, it is a certainty
that if any group in our culture has developed
a degree of literacy in the new communications
media, that group would be the students, not
the professors. It is questionable that the
professors are masters of the old technology—
namely, reading and writing. But even if they
are, the fact remains that they are illiterate
in the language of most of the electric-elec-
tronic communications media. This fact, again,
all by itself, and in the most traditional way,
disputes their position in the hierarchy of
an educational institution. For there is no
more traditional function of a teacher than
that of educating the young to be competent in
the uses of the major media of communications in
their society. When the young know more about
this than their elders, you have a revolutionary situation on your hands.

Another meaning of "smarter" is that the
professors represent a system of values and a
life style that is morally and socially valuable, and which they are capable of communicating with clarity and conviction to the young.
Well, then, what is it that they, the pre-
servers of culture, have to communicate? What
do our professors have to tell us that is decent, and humane, and worth perpetuating? Will
they ask us to be proud that there is an American flag stuck on the moon? Will they tell us

that the 80 billion dollars a year spent on
weaponry is for the purpose of making the
planet safe for democracy? Will they tell us
that Communism is bad? That booze is better
than pot? That cleanliness and short hair are
next to godliness? That we should save our
money and work hard? That Shakespeare was a
great writer? That marriages are made in
heaven? That technology or bureaucracy will
save us all?

Well, we don't want to hear all that crap—
and I do not just refer to the 5 or 10 per cent
of us who say so, loudly. There are many ways
to turn your masters off, and one of them is to
remain quiet and think of something else. You
see, there is another silent majority—one that
Nixon and Agnew haven't mentioned. I mean those
students whose protest takes the form of the
put-on, a kind of benign neglect of the rhetoric of their professors. They show up. They
sit quietly. They do their assignments. But
they are listening to the sound of a different
drummer. (It used to be Ringo Starr.)

So, what I am saying is that our colleges
are at present based on the assumption that
professors can do something important that our
students cannot do; that they know something important that our students do not know; that they
believe something important that our students do
not believe. I say this is mostly false—from
which you are likely to conclude that I think
students are smarter than professors. But if
you do, you are wrong. Our professors do not
know what to do with themselves and their students—that is true enough. But our students
stand roughly in the same position. The world
is no less confounding to us than it is to you.
We are perhaps less burdened by old knowledge
and values than you, but we have not yet formu-

lated useful new ones. We are also, understandably, more frantic than you about the future,
and possibly less accustomed to frustration. We
are surely unskilled in many of the competen-
cies that the present requires, and we are almost completely lacking expertise in the most
critical survival skill of the coming era—
namely, the ability to control the direction
and speed of change. So, to say that professors
are not smarter than students is not to imply
the opposite, but to imply a parity of ignorance—a situation all the more painful because
the twenty-first century is closing in so fast
on all of us.

The first step in reconstructing our colleges is to admit this equality of ignorance,
and the second step is to start <u>acting</u> as if we
knew it. This will make possible the third
step, which is to begin inventing alternative
arrangements for reciprocal education. There
will then be plenty of time for the fourth
step, which is to determine which of our new
arrangements works best.

Now, I have no way of knowing if you think
it sensible to advance with me now to Step
Three. You may believe that you ought still to
be the master in these matters; that your
skills, values, and knowledge are what the
young require to cope properly with the Third
Millennium. If you do, what I am about to suggest probably won't make much sense, unless you
are willing to suspend quite a lot of disbe-
lief. So, if my remarks so far have seemed
wrong-headed to you, then <u>please</u> at least
<u>pretend</u> for a little while that what I have
been saying is more true than false. What sort
of college could we come up with?

The first alternative I have to suggest
even the faculty of a college ought to like. It

would require that everyone on the faculty take a sabbatical leave, beginning the second week of the fall semester and lasting until June. During the first week of the fall semester, the president of the college would explain to the students that all the facilities of the school will be turned over to them—including classrooms, laboratories, gymnasiums, dorms, cafeterias, and the like. The college would pay the maintenance staff, and would insure that electricity, telephones, and other vital services remain operational. The college would also pay the faculty and meet all other financial commitments. During the first week, the students would have an opportunity to meet with faculty members, largely for the purpose of finding out what useful things the faculty knows. These meetings can be supplemented by a directory which lists the address and phone number of each faculty member, along with a statement of what he thinks he can contribute. The faculty would then be free to leave, with assurance given the students that any member will be available to them for whatever professional services the students think are needed. Then, the students would try to run their own college for the year.

As radical as this sounds, I can think of no idea that would more quickly help to close the generation gap. For instance, with the faculty gone, the students would be forced to face and solve administrative problems for which, at present, we show mostly contempt and little understanding. With the faculty gone, the students might have a chance, for the first time, to participate authentically in a democratic and open-ended structure, which is something all their professors want them to learn how to do—or so they say. But most important, the students would be forced to go through the process of trying to decide <u>what's worth knowing and how best to get to know it.</u> There isn't anything more a student can ever ask of a college education than that it give him or her an opportunity to grapple with those questions, right?

If the faculty knows many useful things, the students will discover this quickly, and make the faculty an integral part of their college. If the faculty does not know many useful things, perhaps it will learn some. Neither I nor anyone else has much of an idea of what the students would come up with. Perhaps the same thing we presently have. Perhaps something worse. But it is a chance worth taking, especially if you will keep in mind J. Robert Oppenheimer's observation that there are kids on the street who could solve problems in physics that he could not, because they still retain modes of perception that he had lost long ago. In other words, what this experiment would bring, at its best, is not "curriculum reform," but new modes of perception and thought about education.

But if that suggestion strikes you as bizarre, here is another one, somewhat less drastic, that has been tried with success at the Graduate School of Education at the University of Massachusetts. Keep the faculty on campus, but make the process of "education reform" the content of all their courses. In this way, both professors and students would be asking in every course, Why should a reasonably sane person study this "subject"? In my opinion, this is the only question worth asking in a college course anyway, for the simple reason that if a subject like American history or Elizabethan drama is worth studying at all, you have a whole lifetime in which to study it. The assumption that you can study American history in a fifteen- or thirty-week course is ridiculous on the face of it. What professors can help us to do is not "study" a subject, but entertain questions on what it might be good for. If professors and students were doing that, there would be no need for conferences on curriculum reform, because all your courses would amount to a perpetual process of curriculum reform.

Some people are too attached to the idea of subjects to risk this sort of thing, so here's another suggestion which, in a seemingly less hazardous way, might help to renew the present system in colleges. This suggestion has been made by John Holt in reference to public schools, but I think it would apply even more directly to colleges. Let's build a school on the same model as a public library. That is, the assumptions about the learning process would be the same. For instance, a public library has no admission requirements, no syllabus, no curriculum, no grading system, no Dean's List, no competition, and no tests. People are free to come and go as they please, to read whatever they wish for as long as they feel it useful to do so. Yet it is said that even in such a non-coercive, unregulated structure, it is possible for one to become educated. The principle seems to be quite sound: People go to a library when there is something there that they want or might possibly want. They do not go when there is nothing there they want. Why not have a college based on this arrangement? It is true, of course, that a college offers contacts mainly with people, rather than only with books, but that need not be a disadvantage. People are at least as interesting as books. And it is well within the limits of human potential for professors to create a situation in which students can come and go when they wish, to find whatever they seek. In such a school, all existing offerings would remain, at first, but nothing would be required. The professors would soon discover what their students want to learn, how they want to learn it, and from whom they want to learn it. And that's what education reform is all about, isn't it? Not what is better for you, but what is better for your students.

Now, if <u>that</u> idea seems precarious, here's one that's even more dangerous: Make our school into an institute for social action. Organize the students into teams, each team focusing on the investigation of some social problem. There would be no courses in such an arrangement. Instead, the curriculum would be whatever the students have to do in order to understand the problem they are studying and to offer possible solutions to it. This arrangement is being given a great deal of attention by high schools as well as colleges, especially as it becomes increasingly obvious that adults tend to be incompetent in solving contemporary problems and that students are a rich source of potential help to them. Thoreau made this point in <u>Walden,</u> when he said that "Students should not play life, or study it merely, while the community supports them at this expensive game, but earnestly live it from beginning to end. How could youth better learn to live than by at once trying the experiment of living?" The potential of this alternative is almost unlimited. At Cornell, students are investigating ways of preventing the further pollution of our environment. At NYU, students are monitoring the content of the mass media. The City University of New York is planning a college whose students will mainly be engaged in solving problems of urban life. In September, in a high school not far from here, students will be organized to investigate such problems as crime, drug abuse, and race relations.

Now, I could propose other possibilities for school reform, such as a college modeled on the Woodstock Festival, or the British Infant Schools, or Esalen Institute, or even the Constitutional Convention. But I will spare you any further elaborations, largely because you can invent alternatives as well as I, once you proceed from the assumptions that professors are not necessarily smarter than their students, that both are equally burdened by ignorance, and that both must be equally adventurous in experimenting with the future. If you get to believe that, you will also come to accept as natural that a school based on trust is better than one based on control, and that a school based on questions is better than one based on answers.

I want to close with a few short statements about what I have been saying and the process of renewing education. The first statement is that no curriculum change is worth a damn thing unless the roles of teacher and student are changed. Adding new courses does not change roles, it perpetuates the old ones. The second statement is that there is nothing impractical in any of the suggestions I made. There is a difference between what is unusual and what is impractical. My third statement is that all substantive change—whether it be of institutions or of personal beliefs—derives from changing one's metaphors for what one is doing. And that, in my opinion, is perhaps the most serious obstacle to education change we now face. It is extremely difficult to conceive new

metaphors for learning—far more difficult than
it is to proclaim that the old ones are inadequate. But I think we can do it, if we stop
thinking of each other as natural enemies. As
I said before, it's noisy at the barricades,
and even in moments of quiet we don't seem to
hear each other. Can we get together? Can we
start something? Please let me know.

Sincerely,

THE LETTER YOU JUST READ— IT CAN BE USED, WITH A FEW MODIFICATIONS, BY ANY HIGH SCHOOL STUDENT WHO WANTS TO WRITE TO A TEACHER. BUT FIND A PLACE IN IT FOR THE FOLLOWING QUOTATION:

"There are *no* facts which *everyone* needs to know—not even facts of the first historiographical magnitude. What real difference can knowledge of the fact of the fall of Babylon or Byzantium make in the daily life of anyone except a professional historian? Facts, discrete facts, will not in themselves make a man happy or wealthy or wise. They will not help him to deal intelligently with any modern problem which he faces, as man or citizen. Facts of this sort, taught in this way, are merely empty emblems of erudition which certify that certain formal pedagogical requirements have been duly met. If this method is mistaken for the marrow of education, serious damage can result."

DAVID HACKETT FISCHER,
Historians' Fallacies:
Toward a Logic of
Historical Thoughts

EGO TRIPS

This will be short and unsweet. All human behavior, even among paranoid schizophrenics, is purposive. In most cases, at least with healthy people, the purpose of our behavior is to *enhance* our survival—physical, psychological, symbolic, or whatever. For this reason, we are all on ego trips. We want to make ourselves feel better. Therefore, the charge that someone is ego tripping is a tautology, and in any case irrelevant. The question is not, is he or isn't he ego tripping, but rather, is his particular ego trip helpful to other people or not?

"Busting out ain't no good, Gents! . . . If we're gonna get changes here we'll do a lot better working within the system!"

Action as Rhetoric

⊰ • ⊱

By and large, it has been salutary that young people have become sensitive to what is called rhetoric. Rhetoric is taken to mean words that have no application to the realities of a situation, or, in some cases, no correspondence to the realities of *any* situation. When words are being evaluated in these terms, that is good crap-detecting. But it is not generally acknowledged that an action—for example "liberating" a building or office—is also a form of rhetoric. Sometimes, you hear an overwrought revolutionary say, "We've had enough rhetoric. Let's do something!" But the something that is done may have little or no application to the realities of the situation, and therefore becomes an extension, in a different form, of the empty rhetoric he is trying to be rid of.

Actions are like words in this respect: They may lead you toward or away from what you want to accomplish. Or they may leave you standing in the same place. Actions are not necessarily better than words. It all depends on what you're doing and what you're saying, and what the consequences are.

In pointing this out, we do not mean to denigrate the actions taken by many students on campuses throughout the country. It is perfectly clear that student demonstrations, protests, and strikes have created a setting in which effective renewal of educational processes has become possible. We mean to say that a strike can be as unproductive as a speech, if there is no realistic plan to transform either into an authentic change of procedure.

Which leads us into the subject of TALK,
and since so much talk can be characterized as bullshit,
it might be helpful for us to run down

The Varieties of Bullshit

of which there are so many that we couldn't hope to mention more than a few, and elaborate on even fewer. We will, therefore, select only those varieties that have some transcendent significance.

Now, that last sentence is a perfectly good example of bullshit, since we have no idea what the words "transcendent significance" might mean—and neither do you. We needed something to end that sentence with, and, since we did not have any clear criteria by which to select examples, we figured this was the place for some big-sounding words. Thus, we have our first variety of bullshit—what some people call *pomposity*.

Pomposity is the triumph of style over substance, and generally it is not an especially venal form of bullshit. It is, however, by no means harmless. There are plenty of people who are daily victimized by pomposity in that they are made to feel less worthy than they have a right to feel by people who use fancy titles, words, phrases, and sentences to obscure their own insufficiencies. Many people in the teaching business dwell almost exclusively in the realm of pomposity and, quite literally, would be unable to function if not for the fact that the industry has made this form of bullshit quite respectable. With the possible exception of the profession known as psychology, education uses more pompous language than any other. If you have some doubts about that,

[35]

go read a syllabus. Or a college catalogue. Or a college president's speech.

> **Rule #1:** If an idea cannot be expressed in language that a reasonably attentive seventh-grader can understand, someone's jiving someone else. (Cf. I. A. Richards, and *How to Read a Page*.)

Generally speaking, pomposity is not a serious affliction among young people, although there are some signs that it is increasing. Attempts by some "spokesmen" of the "youth culture" to explain the appeal of LSD or Indian philosophy have provided us with rich examples of bullshit and, at times, have even been reminiscent of explanations given by English teachers of why *Silas Marner* is still required reading in many schools.

A much more malignant form of bullshit than pomposity is what some people call *fanaticism*. There is one type of fanaticism of which we will say very little, because it is so vulgar and obvious. We are referring to what is called bigotry. With a few exceptions, most people know that statements like "Niggers are lazy" or "Fat Japs are treacherous," or "Students are bums," are virulent and ignorant, and are not to be taken seriously. We only want to remark here that some of us who should know better have been slow to recognize that at least as much bigotry is generated by Eldridge Cleaver as by, say, Lester Maddox. Statements like "Cops are racist pigs" make no more sense than any other form of bigotry. And we would include in this the statement that "black is beautiful." We realize that the phrase is intended as an antidote to at least three hundred years of white people's saying the opposite, but, like "blacks have natural rhythm," it attributes characteristics to people solely on the basis of the color of their skins. And *that* is bigoted bullshit, no matter who it comes from or how righteous his cause. The great proletarian revolution will be hastened, not retarded, by acknowledging that, as the color of one's skin does not confer any vices, neither does it confer any virtues.

But there are other forms of fanaticism that are not as bigoted—so obvious—and, therefore, perhaps more dangerous. One of them is Eichmannism. Eichmannism is a relatively new form of fanaticism, and maybe it should be given its own place among the great and near-great varieties of bullshit. At this point, we would judge it to be a branch of fanaticism, because the essence of fanaticism is that it does not admit even the possibility of an alternative point of view, and has almost no tolerance for any data that do not confirm its own. Eichmannism, then, is that form of bullshit which accepts as its starting and ending point official definitions, rules, and categories, without regard for the realities of particular situations. It is also important to say that the language of Eichmannism, unlike other varieties of fanaticism, is almost always polite, subdued, and sometimes even gracious—although in a plastic sort of way. A friend of ours actually received a letter from a mini-Eichmann which began, "We are pleased to inform you that your scholarship for the academic year 1968–69 has been cancelled." In other words, Eichmannism is especially dangerous because it is so utterly' detached. That means, among other things, that some of the nicest people turn out to be mini-Eichmanns. When Eichmann was in the dock in Jerusalem, he actually said that some of his best friends were Jews. And the horror of it is that he was probably telling the truth, for there is nothing *personal* about Eichmannism. It is the language of rules and regulations, and includes such logical sentences as, "If we do it for one, we have to do it for all." Can you imagine some wretched Jew pleading to have his children spared from the gas chamber? What could be more fair, or more neutral, than for some administrator to reply, "If we do it for one, we have to do it for all."

Rule #2: *Everyone* is potentially somebody else's Eichmann. So be careful.

Rule #3: Everyone is *already* somebody else's Eichmann. You weren't careful enough.

There are some other varieties of bullshit that require more than a word or two of explanation, and one of them is what may be called *inanity*. This is a form of talk which plays a large but relatively harmless role in our *personal* lives. But with the development of the mass media, inanity has suddenly emerged as a major form of language in public matters. The invention of new and various media of communications has given a voice and an audience to many people whose opinions would otherwise not be solicited, and who, in fact, have little else but verbal excrement to contribute to public issues. Many of these people are entertainers, such as Abbie Hoffman, David Susskind, John Wayne, Barbara Walters, and Joe Garagiola. Before the communications revolution, their public utterances would have been confined almost exclusively to sentences composed by more knowledgeable people, or they would have had no opportunity to make public utterances at all. Things being what they are, the press and air waves are filled with the featured and prime-time sentences of people who are in no position to render informed judgments on what they are talking about and yet render them with élan and, above all else, sincerity: like Abbie Hoffman on the sociological implications of drugs, Barbara Walters on educational innovation, Johnny Carson on campus unrest, and David Susskind on anything.

Inanity, then, is ignorance presented under the cloak of sincerity, and it differs from the next variety of bullshit—namely, *superstition*—in that superstition is ignorance presented under the cloak of authority. A superstition is a belief, usually expressed in authoritative terms, for which there is no verifiable, factual basis. Like, for instance, that the country in which you live is a finer place, all things considered, than other countries. Or that the religion into which you were born confers upon you some special standing with the cosmos that is denied other people. Or that young people are more sincere and loving than old people. If you think you are not susceptible to this form of bullshit, perhaps you will be willing to ask yourself, On what evidence do you suppose you could do a better job at education than your teachers?

The teaching business has generated dozens of superstitions. Among the more intriguing of these are the beliefs that people learn most efficiently when they are taught in an orderly, sequential, and systematic manner; that one's knowledge of anything can be "objectively" measured; and even that the act of "teaching" significantly facilitates what is known as "learning." By far the most amusing of all our superstitions is the belief, expressed in a variety of ways, that the study of literature and other "humanistic" subjects will result in one's becoming a more decent, liberal, tolerant, and civilized human being. Whenever a professor of

[38]

literature alludes to this bullshit in our presence, we think of the minister of propaganda for the Third Reich and the ideological head of the Nazi Party, Dr. Joseph Goebbels—who at the age of twenty-four received his Ph.D. in Romantic Drama at the University of Heidelberg. Sometimes we even think of the professor of literature himself, and wonder if he would dare to offer his own life as an illustration of the benefits that will accrue from humanistic studies.

There are, as we said, dozens of other forms of bullshit, including several varieties we have been using in this discourse. Perhaps our most obvious one is what might be called *earthiness*— which is based on the assumption that if you use direct, off-color, four-letter words like *crap* and *shit*, you somehow are making more sense than if you observe the proper language customs. Earthiness is the mirror image of pomposity, and, like it, rarely advances human understanding. It is, nonetheless, a serious affliction among many young people, who have somehow got the impression that earthiness is the natural mode of expressing sincerity or honesty or candor. But they and everyone else will probably survive that superstition.

There is some question, however, as to whether we can survive *sloganeering*. Sloganeering is the last variety of bullshit we will discuss, and in many ways it is the most serious. Sloganeering consists largely of ritualistic utterances that are intended to communicate solidarity. The utterances themselves may have meanings quite contrary to those the sloganeers intend—as in the expression "Power to the People." Very few sloganeers who use this expression could possibly want "the people" to have all that "power," since a majority of the people in this country, were it in their power to do so, would probably put an immediate end to most campus dissent, women's liberation, black activism, and other troublesome political movements. What "Power to the People" really means is "Power to *Our* People." The slogan "Free All Political Prisoners" is roughly in the same category. People who use it usually do not mean to include James Earl Ray or Sirhan Sirhan. They mostly mean, "Free Those Political Prisoners Whose Politics We Favor."

The major problem with sloganeering is that it is a repudiation of thought, and may even represent nothing more than an assertion of religious conviction. There is, after all, not much difference between "God bless you!" and "Right on!" so far as their *function* is concerned. Of course, there is nothing wrong with religious utterances, particularly when their purpose is to signal to someone else that you are a member of a certain sect. But when such utterances are used to simulate an idea, they are bullshit, pure and simple, and do nothing to advance any cause. When a "revolutionary" is inclined toward sloganeering, he is more of an obstacle to than an agent of change.

Now, a soft revolutionary has to be an expert in crap-detecting. This does not mean that he foregoes using bullshit. There are many occasions when the best antidote to someone else's bullshit is another variety of bullshit. To use or not to use bullshit is a matter of tactics. To know *when* it is being used, by yourself or someone else, is a matter of expertise. What follows, then, is our version of a mini-course in crap-detecting. The course, as you will see, consists of a few statements—and a lot of questions. (This reflects our belief that it is harder—not impossible, but harder—to bullshit in the interrogative than it is in the declarative.)

STATEMENTS

One man's bullshit is often another man's catechism. (This means that everything one says about bullshit is relative to one's value system. The universe takes no position on bullshit. Crap-detecting is only partly a matter of technique. It is also an expression of your own values.)

At any given time, the chief source of bullshit with which you will have to contend is yourself.

Almost nothing is about what you think it is about. (With the possible exception of those encounters that Fritz Perls calls "intimacy," all human communications have deeply imbedded and profound hidden agendas. Most of the top layer of conversation can be assumed to be bullshit of one variety or another.)

Far and away the most prolific sources of bullshit, after yourself, are idealists. (An idealist usually cannot acknowledge his own bullshit because it is in the nature of his "ism" that he must pretend it does not exist. Anyone who is devoted to an "ism"—fascism, communism, capitalism, youthism, Americanism, etc.—probably has a seriously defective crap-detector, and may be extremely dangerous to other people. This is why it is frequently better to deal with a corrupt man than with an idealist. If you doubt this, keep in mind that, murder for murder, General Westmoreland makes a mafioso look like a flower child. Another way of saying this is that all ideologies are saturated with bullshit—and a wise man will observe Herbert Read's advice: Never trust any group of people larger than a squad.)

QUESTIONS

(which an expert crap-detector keeps in mind when someone is trying to communicate with him, or vice-versa, or when he is trying to communicate with himself.)

Why are these things being said to *me? Are* they being said to me, or to some category of people which I am assumed to represent?

What are these remarks intended to make me feel? Will the feeling be good for *me* or for the person talking? Is the feeling appropriate to the situation? If it isn't, do I *need* to feel a certain way at this time? Can there be *anything* said that does not carry with it some intended feeling?

In what circumstances do *I* talk to people as if they were categories? Are my reasons for doing this any good? Good for whom? Good for what?

What words am I in love with? Where did my affection for them originate? How justified is it in this context? What words am I afraid of? Why? Can I discount this speaker or his position because he uses those words? Does he mean by them what I mean by them?

How do I know that what is being said is true? Does it matter if it's true or not? Matter to whom, and for what? What do I mean by "true"?

In what circumstances do I need to believe something even when

I know it is false? Why do I need to believe those things? What do I mean by "false"?

How many things has the speaker left out? Why did he leave them out? Why did he include the things he included?

Why did the speaker choose those particular words, and not some others that are roughly synonymous? Would I be reacting in the same way if he were saying the "same" thing in different words? Is it possible to say the "same" thing in different words? Is it possible to distinguish between the speaker and what he is saying? Am I reacting to what he's saying or to *him*?

How many beliefs do I have for which I have no basis in fact? What are they? Which of them do I actually *use* in my life? Would it help me if I could get rid of them? What kinds of evidence do I respect most?

Are these remarks intended to be taken literally or metaphorically? How can I know or find out?

Are there things I would like to say but can't put into words? Why?

Do I find I am changing my mind even as I speak? Should I acknowledge this? If I could say it over again, what would I change? Why? Could I say it better? What makes me think so? What do I mean by "better"? Better for what?

Am I listening to what the speaker is saying or to what *I* want to say? Am I hearing what he's saying or what I *want* to hear him say?

Is it possible for someone else's words to make me change my mind? If not, is this good or bad? What do I mean by "good" or "bad"? If so, in what circumstances might this occur?

Why am I saying these things to this person? How many different messages am I sending to him? How many different messages is he sending to me? Which messages are most important to me? What am I trying to cover up? Why?

*If you have to deal
with some real right-wingers,
lay this one on 'em:*

"Is it not ironical that in a planned society of
controlled workers given compulsory assignments, where religious expression is suppressed,
the press controlled, and all media of communication censored, where a puppet government is
encouraged but denied any real authority, where
great attention is given to efficiency and character
reports, and attendance at cultural assemblies is
compulsory, where it is avowed that all will be
administered to each according to his needs and
performance required from each according to his
abilities, and where those who flee are tracked
down, returned, and punished for trying to escape—in short in the milieu of the typical large
American secondary school—we attempt to teach
'the democratic system'?"

ROYCE VAN NORMAN,
Johns Hopkins University,
"School Administration: Thoughts on
Organization and Purpose"
Phi Delta Kappan 47:315–16,
February 1966

[43]

138 QUESTIONS

As we said earlier, before you can start changing a system—*any* system—you need to have a pretty firm grasp on what the system is and how it functions. You also need to be pretty specific in identifying what's wrong with the system, and the directions in which change should go. Now, that's not easy to do. The most significant features of a system tend to be those that are most familiar and obvious. But those are the very features that we habitually overlook, precisely *because* they are familiar and obvious. What we need, then, are some strategies for making those features of a system visible, and therefore subject to analysis, criticism, and change.

One way to see something "new" in a familiar pattern is to change the point of view from which you're looking at it. The most effective strategy we've found for making visible the purposes, underlying assumptions, values, structure, and effects of school systems is to look at them, *not* from the point of view of participants in the system, but from what we call "the anthropological perspective." This strategy requires you to imagine something like this: You have just dropped by parachute into the middle of Hometown, USA—a place you have never seen or heard of and know nothing about, except that it is populated by a strange people with a culture apparently unlike any other on the planet. You are the first contact the world has ever had with the Hometowners, and you want to find out as much as you can about their culture: the purposes of their systems and activities, the values they apparently cherish, their underlying assumptions about human behavior, the rules that govern their systems, the roles assigned to different people in their systems, the responsibilities of different people, the rights granted different people, the restrictions placed on different people, the rituals they practice.

Unfortunately, you somehow arouse the natives' suspicion two or three hours after landing in the settlement, and they confine you to a special building, or group of buildings, which, you discover shortly after, are used in some way to train the young in the ways of the culture. Turning disadvantage to opportunity, you decide to learn all you can about the culture of Hometown by carefully observing the ways in which they train their young.

Imagine, now, that your own school or college is the building or campus where you (in your role as anthropologist) are confined. Try to spend the next few days or weeks looking at the situation through the anthropologist's eyes. Below are some of the kinds of questions you might give some thought to.

Where is the school or campus in relation to the community? Central? Peripheral? In what surroundings? Is it easy to reach? Are there locked doors, fences, "No Trespassing" or "Visitors Report To Office" signs, building guards in or around the building? What purposes do they serve? What underlying assumptions do they suggest about the relationship between school and community? about the relationships between young people and adults? about the relationship between young people and school?

What are the architectural features of the school? What kinds of activities does it seem to encourage? What purposes does the architecture seem designed to serve? What attitudes does it communicate toward school and learning?

What kinds of special facilities does the school have? Are there rooms designed for specific purposes? What purposes? What kinds of equipment does the school provide for athletics? for entertainment? for other purposes? Can you make any inferences about the kinds of activities the school and/or community values most?

What is the interior decoration of the school like? Is it clean? bright? colorful? airy? comfortable? What assumptions about school and learning does the interior decoration reveal?

What are the classrooms like? What kind of furniture do they contain? Is it comfortable? Do teacher and students have the same or different furniture? How is seating arranged? What lines of communication does the seating arrangement suggest? What assumptions about teacher/student status does the furniture and arrangement suggest? What kinds of behaviors does the classroom seem to encourage? What assumptions about teaching and learning behavior does the classroom suggest?

What kinds of objects decorate the walls of the classrooms, the halls, the auditorium? Pictures? What about? Signs? What do they say? Flags? Trophies? Mottos? What kinds of ideas, people, activities does the school seem to honor in such decorations?

What are the rules of the school? Is attendance mandatory?

What purpose-do the attendance rules serve? What assumptions about the relationship of parents to the education of their children do the attendance rules suggest? What assumptions about the attitudes of students toward school do the attendance rules suggest? Does the school have rules for dress? What purposes do they serve? What attitudes toward young people do they reveal? What assumptions about learning do they suggest? What do the rules of the school communicate about the attitudes of school administrators toward the students? about the kinds of behavior the community values and deplores?

Who or what poses most of the questions in the classroom? The teacher? The textbook? The students? Do the students raise any questions at all? In what circumstances?

Who decides what issues will be discussed in the classroom?

Who decides what books should be read? Who decides what projects should be undertaken by the students? Who decides what is a "serious" comment?

Once a question has been raised or a problem posed, who or what is responsible for finding or providing the information necessary to answer or solve it?

[46]

Are students usually urged to accept one right answer to a question or encouraged to consider a number of possible answers?

If the students are urged to accept one right answer to a question, who or what is the source of authority? The teacher? The textbook? The students?

Who does most of the talking in the classroom? Who needs permission to talk? from whom?

To what extent are students prodded to question their own statements, attitudes, beliefs?

Do students address most of their statements and questions in class to the teacher or to one another?

Do students listen as attentively to their classmates as to the teacher?

Are the students encouraged to be more accepting or more critical of the views expressed in their textbooks? of the views expressed by their teachers? of the views expressed by their classmates? of their own views?

Are there particular sources of authority or points of view or areas of discourse students are not encouraged to question?

Your answers to the past twenty questions or so constitute a fairly thorough definition of the roles and responsibilities of students and teachers in the classroom. What roles and responsibilities in the culture is the school training students to assume? What attitudes toward authority is the school training students to accept? What attitudes toward their peers is the school training students to take? What inferences can you make about the behaviors the culture values? What assumptions about the learning process underlie these definitions of roles and responsibilities? What forms of government would you expect to find in a culture which trains its young to assume these roles and responsibilities?

[47]

What kinds of information do the students spend most of their time studying? What purposes in the culture might their learning this information serve? Who in the culture benefits by the students' studying this information?

What kinds of activities do the students spend most of their time performing? What habits or skills do these activities develop or reinforce? What assumptions about learning underlie the encouragement of these activities? What inferences would you make about the information and skills the culture values most? On the basis of the information students study and the activities they perform in school, what inferences would you make about the kinds of things the culture expects them to do as adults?

What kinds of models of adult behavior does the school provide? How do the teachers dress? behave? speak? How would you characterize their personalities? What are their interests? What characteristics do they have in common? In how many ways do they differ? Who are the adults who have been invited to speak at school assemblies and club meetings? What do they do for a living? How do they dress, speak, behave? Who are the people pictured in the halls, on the bulletin boards, and named on plaques in the school? For what reasons are they honored? Are there, in the school, any honorary societies to which students are elected by the teachers? If so, what characteristics do the students elected to these groups seem to share? What inferences can you make, on the basis of these models, about the values of the culture?

How are the students organized for instruction? If they are grouped in some way, what seems to be the basis for grouping them? Does the purpose of the grouping seem to be to promote homogeneity or diversity within a given group? What assumptions about learning does the grouping system reflect? What cultural values and attitudes does the grouping system reflect? What kinds of beliefs, values, attitudes, and behaviors does the grouping system promote in students? Are the different groups of students given different kinds of information to study or activities to perform? What assumptions about human beings and human behavior might underlie such arrangements? What cultural purposes might such arrangements serve?

Are the students in this institution screened or selected in some way from a larger group? What seem to be the criteria for screening or selecting them? What assumptions about learning underlie the establishment of those criteria? What cultural values might the criteria reflect? What cultural purposes might the screening process serve? What does the screening process suggest about the function of schooling in the culture?

What kinds of rites and rituals are performed at regular intervals within the institution? What seem to be the purposes of those rites and rituals? What cultural purposes do they serve? What cultural values do they reflect? What kinds of symbols do they involve? What role do students play in their performance? What role do teachers play? Does the community at large take any part? What cultural beliefs do the rites and rituals encode and transmit to the young?

As we said, these questions ought to help give you a pretty firm grasp on what the system is and how it functions. They will certainly help you distinguish between the *stated* purposes and beliefs of educational systems and their *actual* purposes and beliefs.

Some students have used these and similar questions as the basis of a course that they offered to themselves. For example, a group of education students at a New York City college organized an "extracurricular" course they called "The Ecology of Educational Systems." They used questions like these as the "syllabus." The course was so well-attended that its enrollment had to be restricted. One of the outcomes of the course was that most of the students were better prepared to use the values and assumptions of the system to their own advantage.

An equally productive use of these questions is to get parents, teachers, and administrators to think about them. But don't restrict yourself to the questions we've posed. From an anthropologist's perspective, you ought to be able to invent another fifty or so. Why don't you do it now—like on the next page, where we've reserved space for you.

For your questions:

The Declaration of Independence, the Bill of Rights, and Other Sacred Symbols

Any good soft revolutionary tries to exploit to the fullest the Declaration of Independence, the Bill of Rights, and other such documents that most Americans have not read, but which they revere. (To do this is entirely consistent with the Judo [yes, *Judo*] Christian tradition.)

To begin with, since you are probably not all that familiar with the contents of those documents yourself, you ought to take the time to read them. You might make some important discoveries. For instance, although the Declaration of Independence can properly be characterized as inflammatory and revolutionary (hard variety), there is at least one small passage in it that must give pause to anyone who wants revolution of any kind, soft or hard. The passage reads: "Prudence, indeed, will dictate that governments long established should not be changed for light and transient causes; and accordingly all experience hath shewn, that mankind are more disposed to suffer while evils are sufferable, than to right themselves by abolishing the forms to which they are accustomed." This is essentially an argument for political conservatism, but is not, on that account, to be taken lightly. The argument means to say that if you desire a radical transformation of the procedures in some institution, you had better be damn sure that the existing procedures are quite intolerable. And there is a difference between people's *saying* that they are intolerable and really feeling that they are. If you do not make this distinction, you may find yourself without support at a time when you expected others to join you at the barricades or any other place where they are needed.

There is, for example, a type of "radical" student who too easily succumbs to the lures of vacation time—the student who in the spring is enthusiastic about reform, but who is careful to arrange that he or she will have no responsibilities toward that end during the summer. That the summer is a time for vacation and other swell things is part of the system, and even victims of the system are not usually willing to give it up. Jefferson understood this perfectly well: Given a choice between something that is rotten but habitual and something that may be better but is unfamiliar, most people will stick with rotten.

So, the contents of the Declaration of Independence and other revered documents are useful because they can teach, or remind, soft revolutionaries of things that may be awkward but necessary to know. But that is not the main use to be made of them. Their chief value lies in the fact that, for most people, such documents are sacred texts, like the Bible. It is true enough that when people are asked to support particular statements that are found in the Declaration of Independence or the Bill of Rights, the majority refuse. But most people will also repudiate, in the practice of their daily lives, the moral philosophies expressed in the Bible. And yet they persist in believing that reverence toward the Bible is essential to preserving their way of life. It is the same with sacred political texts.

Now, the orthodox hip response to this fact is pained astonishment or, sometimes, ridicule of the perversity of people. But such a response reveals a very limited knowledge of how societies are held together, for it is done largely by myths, by legends, by symbols, by icons, and by other self-serving imagery, including ennobling versions of history. In pointing this out, we are not being cynical, merely descriptive. How else is any social unit held together? As black consciousness has developed, haven't the Panthers (for instance) rewritten history to suit a new and emerging mythology? Don't students invent images of themselves that make them appear rather better than they deserve? Doesn't any individual keep himself together by self-serving remembrances of things past?

Facts, rationality, and objectivity are not the stuff of which solidarity is usually composed. In ancient times, the bearer of bad news would have his head chopped off. If that doesn't tell you anything, read Eugene O'Neill's *The Iceman Cometh*. People do not love myth-smashers, truth-tellers, or symbol-desecrators. And it is too simple to say that men are just perverse. The reasons go very deep, and they are worth talking about.

To get a perspective on the role of symbols and icons in society, let's take, for example, the flag. Why should a man commit violence against someone who spits on a flag? Would the same man commit violence against someone who spits on the ground— which, after all, *is* the country that the flag stands for? What does it mean to say "a flag has been desecrated"? What is a man saying when he tells you that his son "died for the flag"? What is a flag, anyway? If you took a photograph of a flag, then drew a black and white illustration of the photograph, then made a Xerox copy of your illustration of your photograph of the flag, would it still be a flag? Could the image then be "desecrated"?

Most answers to questions such as these begin with the statement that the flag is a symbol. The most common definition of a symbol is that it is an object that stands for something else and whose form has no inherent connection with that which it represents. Words, for example, are thought of as symbols because their forms are entirely arbitrary—as you can tell by looking again at the words you have just read and trying to see if there is any natural connection between the black scribbles before your eyes and the things to which they are intended to refer. Because there is none, and because the meanings you assign to the words are entirely determined by convention, you and we are demonstrating man's most important intellectual capability: his symbol-making process. But there is another type of message, commonly called a *sign*, which also suggests something other than itself, but which *does* have a connection with that which it calls to mind. A dark cloud, for example, is not a symbol of rain, but a sign of it. A cough would be a sign of a cold. Calloused hands, a sign of hard work. Bulging biceps, a sign of strenuous physical activity. We have here connections dictated by the structure of nature, not the conventions of men.

This distinction—between symbols and signs—is more than academic, for it frequently happens that men mistake their own symbols for nature's signs and, as a consequence, inflict upon themselves more misfortune than their normally perilous lives require. An engagement ring is a *symbol* of intent to wed, not a sign, as more than one girl has discovered too late. And as many a bridegroom has discovered, also too late, a white wedding gown is not a sign of chastity but, alas, only a symbol. On the other hand, with one well-publicized exception, pregnancy is a sign, not a symbol, of non-virginity.

To take an example of a confusion between symbol and sign with more far-reaching effects: Among Hindus, the cow is a sacred animal and not, as for other peoples of the world, a rich source of food. When an object becomes "sacred," it is no longer symbolic. In the eyes of its beholder, there is nothing arbitrary about it; it is completely identified with the idea it represents—like dark clouds and rain. Eliminate one and you eliminate the other. To Hindus, the cow is a sign, not a symbol, and on that account the cow could not easily be replaced by, say, a bird, to represent the same idea—even if the survival of an entire population depended on it.

To take another example: When the British government instituted a calendar reform in the year 1752, the measure required that September 2 of that year be dated September 14. Many Englishmen were outraged because they imagined that their government had deprived them of twelve days of their lives. Consider, for a moment, how you would react if, for the sake of astronomical precision, our government had to date next year 1981. Would you feel that you had "lost" some years, or had been made "older" than in fact you are? The point is, of course, that what we call a calendar is a symbolic system to which the cosmos is largely indifferent, but to which our habits of mind are not. And one of our most complex habits of mind is to transform our symbols into signs; that is, give them a place in nature and, therefore, a life of their own. We invest our symbols with "real" properties and "real" meanings, which is to say we practice magic, every bit as much as the followers of Voodoo. If this were not so, if men were in complete control of their own symbols, there would be no such thing as, for example, "dirty words." There are certain words which cannot be printed in various places, not because the things to which they refer are despised, but rather because the very sight of such words, like certain talismans, produces immediate anxiety and sometimes even trauma. This is man's most profound Faustian bargain: In return for his power to create and manipulate symbols, he permits some of his symbols to recreate and manipulate him. Some would even say that Dr. Frankenstein is more apt a metaphor than Dr. Faust.

So there is in each of us a duality of response to symbols—a yin and yang, so to speak. On the one hand, we respond to symbols as though they were signs, objectify and deify them, then react to them uncritically and with great emotion. On the other, we recognize that it is *we* who codify reality, we who assign meanings to our symbols, we and our relationships to each other that are important, not our symbols. When do we do which? A most important question for any soft revolutionary. On its answers depends the success of many of his strategies. Again, there are many things that are awkward but necessary to know. For example, we know that people tend to invest their symbols with magical powers in circumstances where they do not have much control over their lives. You do not need a witch doctor when you have penicillin. Neither do you need a rabbit's foot when the dice are loaded, and you've loaded them. In this respect it is worth recalling that, to the founders of our country, the symbols of the new nation were understood to be more or less arbitrary and were not invested with much mystery. On July 4, 1776, the Continental Congress appointed a committee, consisting of Franklin, Jefferson, and John Adams, to design a national seal, but their discussions dragged on for years and, in fact, had to be completed by other men. When it was finally decided that the American eagle should be the national symbol, Franklin (who favored the wild turkey) complained that the eagle made its living by stealing fish from other birds, and is a rank coward to boot. No one thought him less of an American for his opinion. No one told him to love the eagle or leave the country. Perhaps because they were in the process of inventing their symbols, the Founding Fathers were not captivated by them. Or perhaps it was because they were in the process of inventing a country. In other words, their energies and sensibilities were being actively employed to alter their circumstances. Their actions were "real" and had practical effects. To a considerable extent, their future as citizens was in their control.

This is a very different situation from the one most Americans find themselves in today. There is a widespread feeling that there is nothing one can actually do to alter the course of events. When people feel this way, they turn inward and act out their opinions through the manipulation of symbols, in the vague hope that their symbolic actions will somehow change reality. The antiwar demonstrator who burns an American flag does not in any way change the situation for the Vietnamese, although his act might permit him to feel he has. In the same vein, "giving one's support to our boys" by wearing a flag in one's lapel does not change the situation for American soldiers, but gives the wearer the feeling that he is "doing" something. A feeling of impotence is perhaps the reason why the hard-hats at construction sites in New York are more preoccupied with the flag than are the hard-hats in the jungles of Vietnam. We massage our symbols when we cannot assuage our circumstances.

We are also, quite likely, being affected by having too many symbols. We in America surely originate and confront more symbolic experience than any other people. Using our advanced technology, we put before ourselves billions of words and images. We are surrounded by them, maybe overwhelmed. Can it be that we are growing to prefer symbols of things to the things themselves? Our magazine ads and TV commercials show us images of men and women who are invariably healthier and more attractive than people we are likely to meet. We regard film stars and TV personalities as our "friends." We have devised computerized boxing matches—that is, fights that have never taken place and never will. Our war is conveyed to us through words and images on a screen. This permits us to have "body counts," to follow troop movements on a map, and to accept "unauthorized incidents" such as that at My Lai. The point is that our media do not in fact bring the *world* into our homes. They bring symbolic representations of the world—a distinction that is becoming increasingly unclear to people. There is a difference between fighting a war through television images and fighting a war in the flesh. Perhaps this is why even antiwar demonstrators are frequently surprised when, during a protest, police or National Guardsmen use real clubs and real bullets. Reality can be an awful shock to people who are too symbol-minded.

But perhaps this is exactly why the flag is being used, these days, so persistently as a surrogate for reality. By thrusting it at each other, people can avoid confronting the real, complex, and ambiguous differences among them. You make your move by putting a flag on your car window. I counter it by hanging the flag upside down. You retaliate by wearing the flag in your lapel. I come back with a peace symbol. You destroy my peace symbol. I spit on your flag. The entire process is not unlike a parlor game, such as *Risk* or *Stratego*. No explanations need be given, no inquiry into each other's thinking, no justification for any of our actions. The symbol *becomes* the entire response.

It is also possible that our current obsession with the flag reflects our anxious awareness that we may *not* be "one nation, under God, indivisible," but many nations, under many gods, greatly divided. Maybe the war has not polarized us, as so many say. Perhaps it has simply made us more aware of how different we are in life styles, aspirations, and concepts of government. When people discover that they do not have as much in common as they thought, especially in times of stress, they transform symbols of unity into signs of it, in the hope that these icons will, if nothing else, produce the same reactions in everyone. Enforcing similarity of behavior toward symbols, such as insisting that everyone salute the flag or say the Pledge of Allegiance, creates the illusion of similarity of feeling when, in fact, there is none. As a general rule, the more one senses diversity of feeling and opinion, the more one tries to enforce "reverence." But it is also important to remember, to paraphrase Shaw, that the man who worships a symbol and the man who destroys one are both idolators. To burn a flag is to invest it with as much reverence as to kneel before it. One does not go through an elaborate ritual of "desecration" if one believes that the object is, after all, only a piece of cloth. In other words, those who wave the flag and those who pull it down may well be expressing the same anxiety over their discovery that they are strangers in a land stranger than they supposed.

Finally, we need to say that in times of rapid change people commonly attempt to stabilize reality by fixing and fixating on their symbols. We try to hold back the dawn by calling it yesterday. Because in America we are undergoing unprecedented changes in our technology and institutions, we are finding it necessary to pretend that much in our lives is still the same. The flag, as well as documents such as the Declaration of Independence, serves as a most convenient sign of permanence and perhaps even of simplicity. For many people, the flag *is* World War II and the unified feeling everyone had then. It is clean rivers and air, tolerable traffic, and everything else that made sense, but went away. Perhaps the flag burners, without knowing it, are burning for many people the connections between what happened before and what's happening now. No wonder, then, the rage that follows.

Now, if you accept this analysis of how men relate to their symbols, how they *need* their symbols, how they are used by their symbols, there are certain judo rules that would naturally follow:

1. Don't "desecrate," in any way, an important cultural symbol.

(As a soft revolutionary, you want to change the system, not infuriate or frighten people. You may be liberated enough to know that the flag is just a piece of cloth, the Bible just a collection of folklore, the Declaration of Independence an inflammatory political tract. But most people are not, and will not be changed much by your attempts to "educate" them. Render unto Caesar that which is Caesar's, and go about your business.)

2. Don't use dirty words.

(The only case we have ever seen of a moderately justifiable use of a dirty word is the bumper sticker which read "Fuck Communism." The signal response most people have toward the first word was more or less canceled out by the signal response they have toward the second. A good judo strategy. But a far better one is to avoid trauma-inducing language in the presence of anyone who might be in a position to advance the cause of change. Lenny Bruce was wrong. You can't talk dirty and influence people.)

3. Don't try to tell people the "real truth" of some matter, especially when it is not entirely necessary.

(In the first place, what you call the "real truth" may only be *your* mythology. In the second place, people don't need to know the "truth" of a matter in order to help in changing something. In fact, they will help more if they can participate within the framework of their "truth." In the third place, and to put it bluntly, nobody likes a smart ass. The last time we mentioned to a group that American civilization was formed from genocide of the native population, insurrection against a legally constituted government, slavery, and exploitation of coolie labor, we were told to go back to Africa—where neither of us comes from.)

4. Don't be too symbol-minded yourself.

(While it is necessary for you to acknowledge that most people respond more deeply to symbols than to "reality," it is also necessary for you to keep your own signal reactions to a minimum. If you do this, you won't be offended by the name-calling done by other people. You won't get into "symbol fights" with others. And, most important of all, you will be better able to tell when you, or someone else, has reached the limits of symbolic expression. For instance, it is not astonishing that a policeman will club someone who shouts "Pig!" to his face. It *is* astonishing—in fact, one of the great psychological mysteries of our times—that the youth who shouts "Pig!" is *surprised* when he gets clubbed. Perhaps he thinks that since an act of *symbolic* violence was good enough for him, it should be good enough for the cop. To take a more relevant example: It is important to know when the use of certain symbols will not help in any way to change the situation. On one occasion, a college student invoked the Bill of Rights to support his contention that students are entitled to due process in suspension cases. The president of the college replied, "I don't want to hear about the Bill of Rights. I'm getting my instructions from the Board of Trustees!" In other words, there are very real power relationships that cannot be influenced by verbal persuasion, even if you have the most powerful symbols of the culture on your side. You have to know when you are and when you are not faced with that situation.)

5. **Nonetheless, whenever possible, use the Bible, the Bill of Rights, the Declaration of Independence, etc., to lend support to your contentions.**

(But be careful to use the appropriate sacred text. There is a joke about a vampire who flew into Patrick O'Rourke's bedroom one night for the purpose of drinking his blood. Remembering the stories his mother had told him, O'Rourke grabbed a crucifix and brandished it frantically in the vampire's face. The vampire paused for a moment, shook his head condolingly, clucked his tongue, and commented genially in the purest Yiddish, "Oy vey, bubbula! Have you ever got the wrong vampire!" The point is that you must become something of an expert in signal reactions; you must be able to predict with a fair degree of accuracy which reactions will be evoked by which symbols. One fairly successful illustration of this technique comes from a group of high school students who prepared a document containing their thinking on the subject of students' rights. The document opened with a quotation from the U.S. Supreme Court in the Gault decision (1967): "Neither the Fourteenth Amendment nor the Bill of Rights is for adults only." There then followed, in parallel columns, quotations from the Constitution and corresponding questions about the rights of students. For example:

Congress shall make no laws abridging the freedom of speech, or of the press. . . .	Why not eliminate all restrictions on student publications? Shouldn't they be given the same protection as *The New York Times* or the *UFT Journal?*
The right of the people to be secure in their persons	Shouldn't school officials, including teachers, be prohib-

. . . papers, and effects . . . shall not be violated. . . .

ited from confiscating any material belonging to students, including comic books, gum, love notes, and even crib notes?

. . . nor shall [a citizen] be compelled to be a witness against himself. . . .

Aren't examinations a violation of this provision?

In this particular case, the students knew well the men they were dealing with. Two members of the school board were super-patriot types who were much inclined to quoting sacred American documents and denouncing those who were insufficiently reverent toward those documents. They were in no position to be flippant about the students' questions, and in fact they were not. The principal of the high school, similarly, was in the habit of worrying publicly about the students' lack of commitment to cherished American ideals. He found himself in the curious position of actually *defending* some of the students' requests. As a result, while the students did not get everything they wanted, they got more than might have been expected.)

6. Use the American flag appropriately.

(To begin with, it is *your* flag as well as *theirs*. The basic point is that the flag may still be the most important icon we have for creating the impression that we are all together. Use it for that purpose. If you do, people will overlook long hair and beads, and may even give your arguments more credence than they deserve. If you must "desecrate" a flag, use the flag of New York City even if you don't live there. No one will mind.)

7. Wherever possible, use biblical quotes in expressing yourself.

7a. In demonstrations, it helps if a priest or minister supports your cause.

8. **Keep in mind that "educated" people are at least as susceptible to icons and signal reactions as the "uneducated."**

   (Despite what teachers and professors like to say, there is no strong evidence that education helps to make people "critical thinkers." In fact, there is some evidence to suggest that education, of the standard variety, makes people more symbolminded, and therefore more susceptible to the manipulation of symbols by others.)

DO IT!

On the heels of the Cambodian incursion and the Kent State shootings, a group of students at Princeton founded the Movement for a New Congress. The purpose of the Movement is to change the nature of the establishment by working for the election of peace candidates to Congress.

As this was being written, the Hatfield-McGovern resolution to set a time limit on the direct use of American military forces in Southeast Asia lost in the Senate by a vote of 55 to 39. While this vote was generally interpreted as a vote of confidence for the Nixon-Agnew-Pentagon war policies, the most important thing to note about it was barely mentioned: the resolution lost by JUST NINE VOTES. If nine more senators had voted *for* the resolution, it would have passed, 48 to 46.

How can students affect the election of public officials? The Movement for a New Congress is doing a variety of things, from making available a detailed record of how every Congressman votes (via computer print-out) to campaigning door-to-door for those whose platforms include a large and *specific* peace plank. It's easy to be "against" the war in general (Johnson was, and so is Nixon), but what we need is something specific—like the Hatfield-McGovern resolution—that members of Congress in particular and members of the society at large can work to support. This includes specific judo-like moves.

During one door-to-door campaign for a congressional candidate, there occurred an extraordinary example of how judo works. The effect was achieved unintentionally, but it would *not* have happened if the student campaigners had been unclear about the purpose of their activities. It would also not have happened if the students had been unaware of the values of those whose opinions and behavior they were trying to affect. Their awareness included, incidentally, knowing that a "hippie" stereo-type, carrying with it very negative reactions, is now epidemic among the "great silent majority." So all the long-hairs and tie-dyeds were put to work on the telephones only.

Because of their sensitivity to their "audience," the students began to do things that they simply would not have taken the time and trouble to do otherwise. (Even though these things were compatible with their own values.) What happened was that two students campaigning door-to-door in a white-upper-middle-class area sat on a curb to eat their lunch out of brown paper bags one noontime. It was a very clean, neat neighbor-hood. When they finished their lunch, they walked half a block down the street to drop their sandwich wrappings and paper bags into a trash basket. Big deal. But some time later, they learned from a woman in that neighborhood that she had voted for their candidate *even though she was a Wallace supporter.* Why? Unknown to them, she had been keeping a wary eye on the students while they ate, and had seen them take the trouble to put their waste paper in a trash basket. If they were good enough to do that, she said, then the man they were supporting was good enough for her to vote for.

We're not saying that this is the sort of thing one can expect to happen, or even that it happens frequently. The point is, though, that what we *do* in specific ways *can* be a most eloquent and effective form of communication and, at the same time, make things better than they are.

Here are some specific things that students have *voluntarily* done recently to help a) to provide much-needed community service, b) to improve the "image" of youth (which, like it or not, needs much improving because of the way the media empha-size the negative connotations of the "hippie" stereotype), and c) to further the soft revolution:

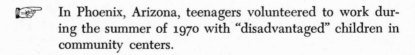

      In Phoenix, Arizona, teenagers volunteered to work dur-ing the summer of 1970 with "disadvantaged" children in community centers.

      In Denver, at the suggestion of Principal James D. Ward, students at the predominantly black Manual High School began a program of building low-cost housing for those who need it most. Working with the Denver Urban Renewal Authority, the students will design, build, and market the homes.

☞ In St. Paul, Minneapolis, and Northfield, Minnesota, lawyers, merchants, and citizens responded to student appeals for funds to support a student lobbying trip to Washington, D.C.

☞ At Glen Cove (New York) High School, the students organized the Glen Cove Youth Council, which prepared a critical analysis of the organization, curriculum, and teaching methods of their school. The report was the result of eight months of research. It included a list of fourteen proposals for change, all of which were perfectly reasonable in view of the information on which they were based. The students emphasized that the fourteen points were NOT threats or demands, but recommendations based upon research that grew out of a genuine interest in improving their school. The report was presented to the superintendent and the school board just prior to the end of the 1969–70 school year.

☞ At the State University at Stony Brook (New York), the students organized a forum in order to discuss different forms of response to the Cambodian incursion and the Kent State shootings in May 1970. More than 250 parents joined an equal number of students in developing alternatives for action. One of the students' mothers even suggested that the parents of college students participate in a general strike to support the students' position.

☞ In Long Beach (Long Island), high school students voluntarily organized a clean-up and repair task force operating out of the Can-Do Poverty Center there.

☞ At Brooklyn College, a group of students got together and talked with the coordinator of volunteer services at Brooklyn State Hospital about what they might do to help the mentally ill. As a result, thirteen teams of six persons each—all volunteers—perform a number of services that the short-handed and overworked regular hospital staff just didn't have the time to do, including taking patients on shopping trips in the community, searching out and getting in touch with relatives, writing letters, and even just talking with patients because no one had had the time to do that in a long, long time.

☞ At the University of Connecticut, four hundred students volunteered to clean up and repair the campus on the heels of a student strike protesting the war in Vietnam. One of the student organizers of the project emphasized that they were not opposed to others organizing, nor did they disagree with their political views. It was just that they thought that if students made a mess they should clean it up.

☞ At Dartmouth College, a professor and student organized the Continuing Presence in Washington. The CPW was set up to maintain a permanent, fully staffed, research-equipped lobby to change U.S. policy in Southeast Asia. CPW plans to recruit parents, alumni, and other eligible voters from labor and business to join the anti-war effort.

☞ In New York City during the spring of 1970, the Voluntary Coordinating Council was organized to provide community services to help children in Head Start programs, to tutor high school dropouts, to work in hospitals, to help in anti-poverty and anti-pollution programs, and to tutor adults in English as a foreign language. Most of the students who volunteered were on summer "vacation."

☞ Students (fifty) and faculty (forty-six) from the Communications Department at Queens College (New York) organized a trip to Washington, D.C., for the purpose of expressing their indignation over the Nixon Administration's escalation of the war in Indochina and the killing of the students at Kent State. While they found little sympathy for their views (which they expected), the experience intensified their determination to work in the fall campaigns for the election of peace candidates, so that views different from the administration's could at least get a fair hearing in Washington.

During the fall semester of 1969, students all over the country organized in a national effort to educate the public at large about environmental problems, staging various events that were "newsworthy" enough to get attention in the media.

At Columbia University, students organized to conduct an educational and rehabilitation program in response to the narcotics problem on campus. They opened and staffed a drug information center on campus that also serves as an emergency station for students on a bummer. The graduating class decided to contribute $1500 to the center, instead of doing something like buying a bronze plaque to commemorate themselves.

On Long Island, students participated in the Nassau-Suffolk School Boards Association workshop on student dissent by role-playing the parts of school board members. School administrators played the roles of students. Student comments included: "I've never realized how difficult it is to be a board member, sitting up front and not knowing what problem you're going to be hit with next." And after posing as a dissident student, the superintendent said, "I'd never realized how frustrating it can be to shout about a problem you're really concerned about and not have anybody listen to you." The process started by having everyone play their "normal" roles, then switching. After playing the others' roles, they got together for a general session to compare notes on how it looked from the others' point of view.

[67]

☞ In New York City, a group of young people formed Frontlash-1970, a student/youth project for grass roots political participation. Their aim is to see to it that large numbers of poor, minority-group, and working-class citizens actually register and vote in elections. Their office is at 120 East 32 Street in New York City.

☛ In Levittown (New York), high school students organized to open a general store they call Middle Earth. One of the store's accountants, a high school sophomore, said, "There are lots of facilities that young people here would like to have, but those things take money. We thought one way to raise money was through a store like this." Almost three hundred students attended organizational meetings, and the County Youth Board helped them to develop plans for different kinds of fund-raising activities. The workers in the store are volunteers. The community —students, adults, and local organizations—donates merchandise to sell in the store.

☞ In California, activist students joined the picket lines with local truckmen during a strike at the Western Carloading Company. One student said, "If we're going to build a radical movement, we have to start moving out of our own community and into the workers' community." While not all of the truckers were initially pleased at being joined by the students, one said, "I have a lot of respect for these kids. A lot of our own guys would have been scared to come down and walk the picket line."

☛ In Brentwood (Long Island), teenagers—all members of the Brentwood High School's Human Relations Council— volunteered to clean up a Head Start play area. One sixteen-year-old said, "We met after the Kent State thing, and we wanted to do something. The kids couldn't stand to sit around and do nothing. We really wanted to help the community." The students organized the Council after the assassination of Martin Luther King.

☞ In Larkspur, California, the seniors at Redwood High School spent the class treasury—$2000—by contributing it to a fund for the purchase of Lower Tubbs Island at the northern end of San Francisco Bay for a bird sanctuary. They said they didn't want to just make another stereotyped gift to the school.

☛ Seniors at Oceanside (Long Island) High School organized their own commencement exercises after school authorities refused them permission to invite Congressman Allard K. Lowenstein (a liberal Democrat who had played a central role in Eugene McCarthy's campaign) to be their commencement speaker. And they did it.

☞ In June 1970, a group of Princeton students worked hard, voluntarily, in a campaign attempt to get a peace candidate elected to Congress. Their candidate lost the election, but the students learned a lot about how to conduct a campaign. They prepared an analysis of their techniques and combined it with a follow-up telephone poll by twenty students who called voters to ask them their reactions to the campaign. The report was sent to the various colleges all over the country that joined Princeton in the Movement for a New Congress. The report is intended to be a primer of effective techniques to be used in political campaigns.

☛ At the University of Michigan, students organized a four-day "teach-in" focusing on environmental problems. Most of the 38,000 students participated in one way or another, even if it was just by wearing an "E-Day" button that said "Give Earth A Chance." The event cost $50,000, of which the university provided $5000. The rest came from student efforts that included selling conservation books and buttons, charging admission, and soliciting contributions from private citizens and industrial organizations.

☞ In Nassau and Suffolk Counties on Long Island, high school students organized the Long Island Students for

Environmental Control. Their activities are wide-ranging —from studying which detergents cause the most water pollution to picketing power companies that heavily pollute the air and water. They have developed long-range plans that include educating the general population in environmental issues so that whole communities can get actively involved in environmental improvement. One student said, "If you get to the people, you are on the way to solving the problem. Even if we just get people to stop throwing beer cans out of cars, we'll be doing *something*."

At Dowling College in Oakdale, Long Island, students met with county policemen just to talk about how things look from their respective points of view. While it was not exactly a love-in, it went well enough for most students and police to agree that more meetings, on a more informal level, would help to minimize misunderstandings resulting from stereotypic thinking on both sides.

In Plainedge, Long Island, after the school budget had been voted down twice in a row, high school students approached the school board president and asked what they could do to help bring the budget up for a third vote. He told them that they'd have to start gathering signatures on petitions. So several hundred of them did. They got more than three thousand signatures, and the school board voted to put the budget up for another vote.

At Camp Paquatuck, operated by the Rotary Club for physically handicapped children, eighteen high school and college students worked all summer with blind, deaf, mongoloid, cerebral-palsied, and other physically disabled children—for little or no money, because the camp is free and their services were needed.

In Mount Morris Park in Harlem, 110 teenagers cleared the trash and weeded a big hill prior to terracing it in order to plant flowers and trees. The action was part of a program run by the Community Thing, a rehabilitation center for addicts. The teenagers were paid $45 a week for five hours' work every day from July to September. The funds came from a state-financed beautification program.

☞ At W. Tresper Clarke High School in East Meadow, Long Island, the student council president, the editor of the school paper, and the president of the school's human rights committee made an appointment with the principal to discuss their views on the ways in which student responsibilities in school affairs could be increased. They made no threats. They just presented their requests in a low key. After an hour's meeting, the principal declined to meet any of their requests, but they'll be back. As the student council president said, "Students don't just go to school; they *are* the school, or at least a significant part of it, and they want to be recognized."

☞ Student leaders from the different colleges that comprise the State University of New York formed a new student association to jointly represent the sixty-seven campuses of SUNY.

☞ At Lawrence High School, a group of twenty-nine students prepared an eighty-page critique of the aims, purposes, and programs of the school, and presented it to the superintendent. As a result, he arranged for discussions to be held between students and faculty. Many suggestions were offered, and some changes were made. Later, twenty-five students produced a fifteen-page report on the results of their efforts.

☞ At San Fernando Valley State College in California, a group of students organized to start an ecology magazine. Since they knew nothing about publishing a magazine, they didn't know they couldn't do it. They managed to get Senator Edmund Muskie, Senator George McGovern, and Representative George Brown of California to serve as contributing editors to their magazine, which they call *Environmental Quality*. Even before they had their first issue laid out, they also managed to line up Ralph Nader, Representative Tom Rees of California, and the president of the Security Pacific National Bank. The motto of their magazine is "If you can see it, you shouldn't breathe it."

In Berkeley, after two weeks of angry demonstrations for a People's Park had gotten them blasted with buckshot, tear-gassed, clubbed, and busted, the young demonstrators figured out that a "soft" approach would be at least less damaging to themselves, if not more fruitful in "liberating" the park. So, they changed their strategy, and 20,000 of them marched—after getting a permit. They smiled and flew kites and balloons and waved flags and stuck flowers in the fence and on cops' helmets and there were no casualties and almost no busts and even the cops smiled.

At San Diego State College, students organized the Educational Movement Center to analyze and describe campus power structures and to serve as a national information dissemination center for student groups interested in educational change. One of its programs is devoted to Power Structure Analysis, in which students are assigned as assistants to administrators. They all meet once a week at the Center to analyze the decision-making process at the institution in which they are working.

And all over the country, students are organizing telephone "hot lines" which teenagers—whether students or dropouts—can use to rap about whatever it is that's bugging them—from pregnancy to being hooked on junk to wanting to locate a crash pad or a commune or whatever. Some teenagers use the hot line just to rap *at* someone who won't start giving them lectures or advice but will *listen* while they talk it out. It is increasingly common for such hot lines to have the telephone number of a source of legal assistance in case of a bust.

☞ Meanwhile, back in Dacca, Pakistan, the students at Brahmanbaria College are fighting for the right to cheat on exams.

That's just a *short* list of some of the things students are doing in an attempt to make things better. They are all real, and they are an indicator of a growing wave of student efforts to do something that makes the right kind of a difference to themselves and to society in general. It isn't easy, and it isn't magic, but, as we said, it beats standing on a corner and yelling "Power to the People!"

HERE IS A WAY
To Triple the Number of Teachers in Our Schools At No Cost Whatsoever to the Taxpayers

WHILE AT THE SAME TIME
Enriching the Education of All Students

AND MAYBE EVEN
Raising the Salaries of Those Already Teaching

Make the curriculum for the senior year in high school a teaching experience. Everyone knows that the best way to learn something is to try to teach it. So, all seniors would be required to teach in the lower grades and junior high school—perhaps the very subjects they have had some difficulty with. If each senior were assigned to teach reading, or math, or science, or whatever, to just six kids, you would accomplish the following:

> *the seniors would learn a great deal more than they would otherwise,*

> *the kids would learn a great deal more than they would otherwise,*

> *the regular teachers would have more time and energy for creative teaching,*

the community would not have to hire so many new regular teachers, and would therefore actually save some money, which it might wish to use for increasing the pay of those already teaching.

If this were done on a statewide basis, you would have a major educational revolution. It won't be. But it can be done by a single school. Maybe yours. Why not propose the idea to your school principal? If he doesn't like it, propose the idea to a member of the school board. If he doesn't like it, begin anyway. After school, in an informal way. Imagine the effect on a community of twenty or thirty or fifty high school seniors' organizing to help grade-school kids learn. Perhaps the best approach is to offer the kids courses that are not available in the regular school: astronomy, guitar, space technology, film, marine biology, photography, etc. Another possibility is to teach skills that the schools are unsuccessful at teaching: writing, reading, etc. With any kind of luck, and some reasonably good promotion, the school establishment ought to get very interested in the project, and will probably accept the idea. Even if they don't, it's a good idea anyway, and it ought to be tried.

Next time a school administrator challenges you to suggest "something better" if you don't like the way things are, tell him about what they're doing in John Adams High School in Portland, Oregon.

HERE'S THE STORY:

Report Hails Oregon High School's Experiment in Free Study

By WILLIAM K. STEVENS

Special to *The New York Times*

PORTLAND, Ore.—The clean-lined, futuristic colonnades, court-yards and skylights of Portland's John Adams High School symbolize a fresh view of how teen-agers should be educated.

Opened just over a year ago on a site south of the Columbia River, it houses what may well be the country's "most important experiment in secondary education," according to the recently published report of a three-and-a-half-year study of American schools commissioned by the Carnegie Corporation.

Adams High seeks to determine whether ordinary teen-agers are willing and able to accept day-to-day responsibility for their own education—planning their own studies, sometimes developing their own tailor-made courses and managing their own time.

Thus a black senior, Don Bilbrew, is free to embark on a two-year independent study of black history in Portland that requires him to make use of the disciplines of sociology and economics as well as history. At the same time he can, and does, study such subjects as Shakespeare, drama, biology and journalism.

And Diane Crane, a sophomore, can branch out from her state-required biology course and undertake an independent study of genetics.

Conceived at Harvard

The Adams experiment is attempting to eliminate what the Carnegie study found to be some of the most damaging features of the typical American high schools: Encouragement of docility and conformity; overregulation of students' lives; and a pallid, uniform curriculum.

The experiment was conceived three years ago by seven young Ph.D. candidates at the Harvard University Graduate School of Education. One of them, Robert Schwartz, 32 years old, is now the principal of the school.

Similar ventures in "free" or "open" education for teen-agers are going on elsewhere, but in relatively small, especially constituted environments with selected or volunteer students. Adams, by contrast, is a regular district high school operating within political and economic realities. Its student body of 1,600 is drawn from all social strata, with a heavy contingent from white working class families. A

quarter of the students are black.

"If the approach works here," says Mr. Schwartz, "it will work anywhere."

Rules Are Few

The Adams approach begins with the proposition that the overall climate of a school may have a stronger effect on student learning than the formal curriculum.

"If you require a kid to have a hall pass you're saying you don't trust him," Mr. Schwartz said. "You then undercut the value of any 40-minute lesson in self-direction."

Except for the fact that students must come to school and participate, and that they must obey civil laws, Adams has few rules and regulations.

Legitimate authority at Adams is held to be rooted in experience and knowledge. Since adults are by and large more experienced than children, it is reasoned, they have a kind of "natural" authority that makes itself felt when an adult deals with a youngster on an equal, respectful footing.

Teachers are viewed as helpmates and colleagues, not dictators. "We try not make decisions for kids," Mr. Schwartz said. "We press the student to confront himself and what he's going to do with his life, and to make responsible choices. We are not permissive."

For many students accustomed to being told what to do, the

pressure to choose has been uncomfortable, even painful. Some students have simply refused to act for themselves or to go to class, but Mr. Schwartz said that a large majority adjusted to the new way of doing things.

Curriculum for Generalists

Students at Adams choose as electives many essentially traditional courses—for example, physics, chemistry, electronics and industrial arts. Often students work independently in such courses, checking with the teacher only when help is needed.

But the pride of Adams's effort at curriculum reform is an interdisciplinary "general education" course set up this way:

Students and faculty are divided into seven "teams," each of which designs its own learning program that will lead students to explore key concepts in the state-required subjects of English, social studies, mathematics and basic science. Typically, a team will do this by focusing on some real-life problem—race relations, for example—that can be attacked through the application of several disciplines.

Thus, a team headed by teacher David Mesirow has begun a unit called "the psychology of self,"

designed to enable students to become surer about their own identities and their relationship to the rest of the world. The team will focus in sequence on politics, students' rights and the process of change; values, advertising and the media; the experience of poverty; the black experience; alternative life styles; and the urban environment of Portland.

General education meets for half a day every day, but a student may skip the group sessions in favor of independent study if he wishes. Should general education spark several students' interest in some particular subject —say, general philosophy—a six-week "mini-course" is organized.

Each student has two free option periods a day, during which he can do anything he likes, or nothing. Some do nothing.

Students choose whether to be given letter grades or to receive a "credit-no credit" rating.

Parents' reaction to the experiment has been mixed.

A survey of students indicated that they considered Adams a "humanized" school. "At least you feel like a person here," said one student. But the same survey found that many students felt the intellectual content of the curriculum should be strengthened.

The New York Times
Monday, October 19, 1970

[78]

"We have changed the environment,
and now we need to change ourselves."

Norbert Wiener, The Human
Use of Human Beings

THE POWER
~ OF ~
INTERRUPTION

To most of us, the ordinary and routine are invisible *because* they are ordinary and routine. Marshall McLuhan was making this point when he noted that "Whoever it was discovered water, you can be sure it wasn't a fish."

Now, most people not only aren't interested in changing the ordinary and routine, they can't even imagine the need for doing so because of the invisibility of the habitual. In order to get people to consider changing something, you have to get them to think about it. In order to get them to think about it, you have to make it visible to them.

One of the objectives of the soft revolution is to make the ordinary visible. One way to make the ordinary visible, curiously enough, is to subtract it. Air is literally invisible, and people tend not to be able to think of it until they don't have any. One way of making ordinary school routine visible to those who unthinkingly accept it is to interrupt it. By *not* doing something that is routinely expected, you can make the routine quite visible to everybody.

At Tufts University, in June 1970, the graduating seniors made their point about how irrelevant they thought conventional commencements are by *not going* to the routine commencement exercises. They had informed their parents and friends about this, but not the school administration. So, came commencement day, there was the dais, full of dignitaries and honorary degree recipients and guest speakers. They faced a quadrangle full of empty chairs. The students held their own commencement, which their parents and friends attended, the next day.

These students did not *disrupt* the ordinary commencement exercises, but they sure did *interrupt* them—simply by not attending. And their not attending probably had a more profound and productive effect on the administration than any kind of disruption they might have attempted.

Of course it took organization on the part of Tufts' seniors to make this strategy work. If you think of the organizing possibilities that lie in the kind of student union we describe elsewhere in this book, and the kinds of interruption such a union would make possible, you can begin to get some sense of the potential of student power. *Not* doing something can be the most effective strategy for applying that power because it is, oddly, the most difficult to cope with. You can't call the cops or the National Guard if students *don't* come to a commencement. It's like Yogi Berra once said while looking at lots of empty seats in Yankee Stadium: "If people don't wanna come, you can't stop 'em."

What changes might occur if, for example, all of the students in a course or college just did not show up to take exams? Or what changes might occur if all students just did not comply with routine clerical procedures, such as filling out IBM cards? Or what changes might occur if all the students in a course just did not ever attend any "lectures"?

Interruption as opposed to disruption can be effected, of course, by *doing* something, too. A group standing up and singing "The Star-Spangled Banner" can interrupt almost any routine procedure. And who could or would want to bust a group of students singing our national anthem? How would a group of hard-hats respond to a bunch of long-haired, hippie-looking kids who are carrying the American flag and singing "The Star-Spangled Banner"?

Another form of interruption consists of doing *exactly* what some authority instructs you to do, but no more. One of us had the experience in the Army of being told over and over, "Never mind trying to think. Just do what you're told. Period." So one night when his tent caught fire, he just watched it burn to the ground. When the first sergeant screamed at him, "Why the hell didn't you put the fire out?" he just said that nobody told him to.

Then, of course, there is Napoleon's great line: Never interrupt your enemy when he is in the process of destroying himself. In other words, there is a time for everything; and more than once in a while there is a time for you to say nothing and do nothing except to watch some piece of nonsense be consumed by its own irrelevance or inefficiency. Or, in other words: Don't just *do* something. Stand there!

Here are some examples of how these principles have been used in actual situations:

A class of high school seniors in California was faced with an exceptionally mean English teacher. They decided to strike back—judo style. So they brought her a bouquet of flowers every week for the whole year. (Flattery, they discovered, will get you everywhere.)

In several colleges and universities, students have responded to being graded by publishing their own evaluations of their professors. The result is that there is more talk than ever, on these campuses, about moving to a Pass/Fail grading system.

Because their college catalogue was typically dull and filled with irrelevant and untrue statements, some students in a freshman composition class wrote their own version of the catalogue, in which they told the truth about courses and how the college actually operates.

Depressed by the filth and disrepair of their "ghetto" schools, high school students in several places have offered to clean them up.

At a university in New York City, students faced the prospect of dull and repetitive lectures by a dull and repetitive professor. So they suggested to him that the course might be enriched by having guest lecturers to supplement his ideas. He agreed, and the students arranged for seven guest lecturers.

At a high school in Connecticut, there existed a rigid dress code, based on the assumption that uniqueness in dress is distracting. So all the seniors handed in identically worded compositions to their English teachers, and identically worded "research" reports to their social studies teachers. They explained that since the school administration felt that uniqueness was distracting, they didn't want to distract their teachers or themselves with individual expressions of opinion.

Bowdoin College in Maine no longer requires an applicant to take the College Boards. Other schools are also considering dumping them. If you don't do anything, the tyranny of College Boards will eventually be ended. As will the New York State Regents Examinations.

FROM

WANTED:
A Humane Education

Which was written by students of
Montgomery County (Md.) Public Schools

A PROGRAM FOR CHANGE

1. Establishment of an ombudsman office, responsible directly to the Board of Education, to investigate and resolve complaints from students.

If the goals and realities of the school system are ever to be brought into line with one another, it is essential that a procedure be developed to deal with instances of questionable treatment of students. Every student in county schools should be informed of the existence and purpose of the ombudsman office, and they should be made to feel free to make use of it without any fear of retaliation. It is important that the ombudsman office not be in the position of having to be defensive about the actions of school administrators and teachers. Ombudsman officials, independent of any such pressures or biases, must take a stance of neutrality and work vigorously to correct the thousands of injustices which occur every year to students who presently have no way of seeking redress.

2. The school system must put an end to intimidation of students through abuse of college recommendations, grades, secret files and "permanent record files" by school officials.

These incidents are often hard to pin down, but students are definitely being blackmailed and intimidated—with varying degrees of subtlety—through use of these documents. Students must be given access to their own files, and must have control over who can and cannot see them. The Board of Education should issue a firm memo to all teachers, administrators and counselors in the county schools emphasizing the Board's disapproval of intimidation and anything short of straightforward dealings with students in these areas. In addition, the ombudsman office for students should work to uncover and eliminate misuse of these files and documents.

3. Students must have an important role in the shaping and implementation of courses. They are also in an excellent position to provide meaningful feedback by providing continuous evaluation of the effectiveness, strengths and weaknesses of their classes.

The school system has "proclaimed" many policies and has made them stick. Teachers should be told that it is essential to have students discuss how courses and classes should be designed and operated. This continual re-evaluation will see to it that classes and courses of study are constantly improved and updated. County school officials determining courses of study must be willing to permit much more flexibility and originality than is presently allowed. Departmental faculty meetings, it should be made clear, are open to participation and input from students. On the individual class level, the successes and failures of the class can be continually evaluated by students and teachers working together and planning together.

4. Student input in teacher evaluations.

Being a good teacher involves many characteristics beyond the ability to keep accurate records, complete forms neatly, "control classes" and receive degrees from graduate school. Whether a teacher is stimulating, creates enthusiasm, is responsive to individual needs and problems of his students, can relate to students (and vice versa) and treats students with respect for their human dignity is all extremely important. Students are in the best position to provide very valuable information in these areas, and it would seem logical to construct a regular system for obtaining such feedback from students.

5. Tension and rigidity must be eliminated from the schools.

Administrators must be made to stop constantly threatening students with arbitrary, almost whimsical disciplinary actions.

This implies a change in attitude; an elimination of the approach which says that to have students expressing themselves, verbally and through interaction, can pose a threat to the "authority" and "order" of the school system. Students are being pressured, threatened and suspended for skipping classes, being in the halls without passes or even possession and/or distribution of literature. A system which has an elaborate policing-system network for keeping students out of the halls and for catching students who choose not to attend classes is perpetuating tension which is absolutely unnecessary, damaging to morale and totally out of place in an institution which says it seeks to encourage learning and exploration.

6. Hiring of educators and researchers to deeply examine what effect the school system has on a student's self concept, creativity, and desire to explore and learn.

Much of the evidence and research in this area, we feel, has already been developed (and is presently being ignored—no doubt because the findings are so very unpleasant). The study mentioned earlier, James Coleman's *Equality of Educational Opportunity*, shows that self concept and sense of control over one's own destiny is much more significant in the development of a child than the many other factors school administrators spend all their time worrying about. The forces which presently destroy a student's self concept and feeling of control over his own fate must be eliminated immediately. We feel it is clear that this is going to have to mean elimination of the disciplinary threats and punishments prevailing throughout the school system, of the clockworklike class schedules and tension created by school administrators and teachers who have been encouraged to emphasize and flaunt their authority.

7. Elimination of letter grades.

This is extremely important. The use of letter grades as the basis upon which the school system is operated sets the tone and patterns of the public school experience. Its destructive effects have already been noted.

In elementary and junior high schools, grades should be abolished immediately and replaced with written evaluations by the teacher. In high school, students should simply receive credit or not receive credit for each course he has taken. In order for the students to get feedback as to how they are progressing, teachers should provide students with written and/or oral evaluations as often as necessary. Students should receive a copy of all written evaluations; a copy could be entered in students' files but should not be released to colleges without student-parent consent.

Transition may seem rather difficult at first. But the benefits will be both immediate and increasingly apparent as students make the adjustment and begin to shake off the bad attitudes and effects of the old system. The natural joy in learning will re-emerge, and hopefully for those starting out in the system it would never be squashed in the first place.

If a complete change is made for all the schools in the county, colleges will have no choice but to consider each applicant from the county on their individual merits; they would be forced to do without grades and class rank in evaluating applicants (there are many other methods of evaluation), especially in view of the reputation Montgomery County enjoys nationally as a school system of unquestionable academic quality.

There are ways if there is the will.

8. Teachers must be encouraged and allowed to respond to the individual needs of their students. This will have to mean fewer regulatory restrictions, more flexibility.

9. Students must be given the ability to exercise control over what happens to them in school. Specifics: The right to transfer out of a course that is not satisfactory; the right to go on independent study at any time; the right to formulate their own goals and how they can best go about achieving them.

10. Rigid periods now being used in county secondary schools must be replaced with shorter and more flexible modules.

Kennedy High School's use of modules—short blocks of time—makes the school more flexible and open to different kinds of activities. There are now no provisions for spontaneous activities; in fact, they are absolutely prohibited. Periods which last 50 minutes or an hour are confining and should be eliminated. Elimination of bells would be a healthy developmen*

11. Students must have a right to print and distribute their own publications, and restrictions should not be set up to impose

obstacles—as has been the case—but rather to provide students with an orderly means of distribution, such as tables in the halls, near doors or in the cafeteria. These requirements should apply equally to all student publications. (The fact that money is involved has been used as an argument against allowing "underground" or unsanctioned papers, but money is always also involved with sanctioned, official student newspapers.)

12. Students have the right to have the freedom to decide what they want to print in student newspapers, literary magazines and yearbooks. Censorship by sponsors or principals, whatever the degree of subtlety, must not be allowed.

13. Outside speakers must be given a chance to speak to students without favoritism or discrimination.

Military recruiters, for example, address assemblies at each county high school every year, but the same right has been refused to groups presenting different or opposing viewpoints. Students must make the decisions to invite speakers and arrange assemblies.

14. The providing of the names and addresses of senior boys to the armed forces must be ended.

The county school system makes a point of its desire to protect students from businesses who get hold of mailing lists of students, yet it provides the names and addresses of senior boys in county high schools to the military. Peace and pacifist groups have been refused the same privilege. The lists should either be available to groups which disagree with the military or should not be released at all.

15. Relevant courses must be developed to meet student interest.

Students should be surveyed as to what courses they would like to see offered, and the results should play a determining role in the direction of course offerings. Racism, urban life, suburban life, drugs, human relations, foreign policy, police-youth relations and civil liberties are a few topics in great need of curriculum development.

16. Students should be free to arrange voluntary seminars to be held during the school day.

If schools are really to become relevant, students must be allowed—indeed encouraged—to set up discussions, hold workshops and seminars, hear speakers who are well-informed about the subjects that interest students. The students should be free to invite speakers and outside authorities to come in and give their views, without the obstacles which presently exist. Schools must come alive. The concept behind the "Experiment in Free Form Education" being tried at Whitman for one week must be integrated into the everyday functioning of the schools. With schools becoming much more individualized, students should be given the flexibility of attending seminars of interest during the school day.

17. Expansion of the range of resources.

Diversified paperback books giving different perspectives could play an important part in widening the scope of thought and exposure in the schools. Textbooks alone are just too limited in coverage and perspective.

18. Informing students of their rights.

The school system should take the responsibility of informing each student of his rights in dealing with administrators and teachers. If the School Board agrees that students do have rights, then it must be willing to make these rights directly known to each student.

19. Restrictions having to do with student dress must be eliminated throughout the county.

20. County seminars in human relations, racism and progressive teaching methods should be held for teachers.

An excellent week of seminars was held by the Montgomery County Public Schools last August for about 100 county administrators. It would be very good if the same sort of program could be set up for the county's teachers.

21. Material thoroughly exploring Negro history must be integrated into classes such as U.S. History and Problems of the 20th Century. Special training should be provided to teachers in order to make them qualified to deal with this very important aspect of American history and society.

22. The School Board should launch an investigation of illegal searches of lockers in secondary schools for drugs and the recruiting by school officials of students to become narcotics informers.

School officials have been known to actively seek and encourage students to become drug informers. The unhealthy atmosphere which such a situation creates should be a matter of concern. We feel the School Board would agree that it is not a desirable situation to have students promoted to act as spies on other students in school. Such activities have no place in an institution of learning.

23. School Board hearings for students.

It is important that school officials come into contact with the concerns of students. The Board could schedule hearings every two weeks at which time students would be invited to testify and voice complaints and suggestions.

24. Student voice on School Board.

The School Board would do well to include representation of students. Every semester the School Board could supervise the election of student representatives from among county high school students, printing a special bulletin for each high school student which would give the positions of each of the students who had volunteered to run for the positions.

"The greatest charity
is to be found among those
who have not observed regulations."

EZRA POUND, Canto LXXIV

THE PUT-ON
IS MIGHTIER THAN
THE PUT-DOWN

If you are working to change something in school and you aren't laughing, or at least smiling, most of the time, you probably need a different strategy.

Never underestimate the power of the put-on. It is very judo-ish, and there is no equivalent for the cleansing ripple of laughter that follows the recognition of the emperor's new clothes.

Pomposity and piousness are commonly used to cloak stupidity. Therefore levity and good-natured irreverence can be used to reveal it.

In any case, if you find yourself morbidly serious in your talk and action about change, you should take time out to think of some funny things to say and do—*not* just for their own sake (although that alone is almost reason enough), but to increase the effectiveness of your efforts.

It's very difficult for someone to get angry at you when they're laughing.

Here's one example of the use of irreverence to reveal irrelevance. Below we have printed in its entirety a test which takes as its model the SAT's. In *this* test, SAT stands for Silly-Assed Trivia. The test was devised by Mr. Terence Patrick Moran, who cheerfully grants us permission to publish it. He also cheerfully grants you permission to use it in any way you deem fit, provided that you do nothing with it that would disgrace his good name. He would prefer that you do something like this: Xerox a few copies and give them to your professors or (high school) teachers. (The answers are given, for your use in grading others, at the end of the test. If you need the answers to feel better about yourself, go back to the beginning of the book and, this time, try to get it straight.) A very few of your instructors (*very* few) will, upon completing the test, immediately cancel the syllabus of their course and try to invent something useful to take its place. A few more will completely change the form of their final exam, or may even cancel it. Most will be amused, but won't do anything. Here are some questions you should address to *them:*

1. Which questions in the test strike you as trivial? Why?
2. How do you know that your standards of significance (or trivia) are better than mine?
3. If I take your trivia test (midterm, final, whatever), would you be willing to take one of mine?
4. Suppose you were willing, and we both passed—or flunked. What would it prove?

Actually, if you have to ask these questions, the point of it all is probably lost, but it might be worth trying anyway.

SAT TEST

Section One: Humanities

Directions: In each of the following, select one of the choices which will make the sentence most nearly correct. Record your answer in the space to the left of the question number.

_____1. A silver bullet ends the life of the principal character in
    (a) <u>Orpheus Descending</u>
    (b) <u>The Emperor Jones</u>
    (c) <u>The Silver Cord</u>
    (d) <u>The Great God Brown</u>

_____2. A silver bullet is used as an identifying symbol by
    (a) The Durango Kid
    (b) Tom Mix
    (c) The Lone Ranger
    (d) Hopalong Cassidy

_____3. Dora Spendow, Steerforth, and Mr. Murdstone are characters in
    (a) <u>Seventeen</u>
    (b) <u>Tom Jones</u>
    (c) <u>Jane Eyre</u>
    (d) <u>David Copperfield</u>

_____4. Titus Moody, Senator Claghorn, and Mrs. Nussbaum are characters in
    (a) "Life With Luigi"
    (b) "Allen's Alley"
    (c) "Amos n' Andy"
    (d) "Out Our Way"

_____5. "Thou shalt see me at Philippi" is the warning given to
(a) Hamlet   (c) Cleopatra
(b) Brutus   (d) Romeo

_____6. "Even he who is pure in heart and says his prayers by night can become a wolf when the wolfbane blooms and the autumn moon is bright" is a warning given to
(a) Clyde Beatty   (c) Lawrence Talbot
(b) Conrad Veidt   (d) Alf Landon

_____7. The term "Kemo Sabe" is associated with
(a) Rudyard Kipling   (c) Zane Grey
(b) Edgar Rice Burroughs   (d) George Trendle

_____8. The term "Malapropism" is associated with
(a) Wilde   (c) Congreve
(b) Sheridan   (d) Shaw

_____9. A novel that presents a picture of clerical life in a cathedral town is
(a) <u>Barchester Towers</u>   (c) <u>Middlemarch</u>
(b) <u>Wuthering Heights</u>   (d) <u>Vanity Fair</u>

_____10. A radio show that presents a picture of theatrical life is
(a) "Helen Trent"   (c) "Mary Noble"
(b) "Stella Dallas"   (d) "Our Gal Sunday"

_____11. The author of "Eclogues, Epitaphs and Sonnets" was
(a) Fulke Greville   (c) Barnabe Googe
(b) Lord Feveral   (d) John Dryden

_____12. Schiller, James, and Dewey are associated with

(a) Pragmatism   (c) Deism
(b) Positivism   (d) Fascism

_____13. Solomon, Hercules, Atlas, Zeus, Achilles, and Mercury are associated with
(a) The Iliad   (c) The Ecumenical
(b) Captain Marvel   Movement
     (d) Socrates

_____14. "Cogito ergo sum" expresses a phase in the philosophy of
(a) David Hume   (c) Ralph Waldo
(b) Rene Descartes   Emerson
     (d) Friedrich
     Nietzsche

_____15. "I think I can, I think I can, I think I can" expresses a phase in the philosophy of
(a) Richard Nixon   (c) The Little
(b) The New York   Engine
     Mets   (d) Norman Vincent
     Peale

_____16. The "Grand Canyon Suite" was written by
(a) Ferde Grofe   (c) Roy Anderson
(b) George Gershwin   (d) Leonard
     Bernstein

_____17. "A Hard Rain's Gonna Fall" was written by
(a) Dylan Thomas   (c) Joan Baez
(b) Woodie Guthrie   (d) Robert Zimmerman

_____18. Of the following, the instrument which is not usually found in a symphonic orchestra is the
(a) oboe   (c) tuba
(b) saxophone   (d) bassoon

19. Of the following, the instrument which is not usually found in a Rock group is the
(a) organ   (c) harp
(b) electric guitar   (d) drums

20. Of the following artists paired with famous works of art, the pair that is incorrect is
(a) Botticelli—The   (c) Durer—
     Sistine Ceiling   St. Jerome
(b) Brueghel—The   in His Study
     Wedding Dance   (d) El Greco—
                         View of Toledo

21. Of the following artists paired with famous works of art, the pair that is incorrect is
(a) Schultz—   (c) Caniff—
     Peanuts   Dick Tracy
(b) Young—Blondie   (d) Capp—L'il Abner

22. "The Disasters of the War" is the name of a series of
(a) paintings by   (c) drawings by
     Rubens   Holbein
(b) etchings by   (d) engravings by
     Goya   Durer

23. "Up Front" is the name of a series of
(a) photographs by   (c) cartoons by
     Grady   Mauldin
(b) etchings by   (d) profiles by
     Picasso   Pyle

24. Of the following, the artist who is best known for developing the "functional use of color" to create form is
(a) Rembrandt   (c) Ingres
(b) Cezanne   (d) Daumier

_____25. Of the following, the artist who is
best known for developing close detail
in illustrations is
(a) Zach Mosley   (c) Chester Gould
(b) George Wunder   (d) Hal Foster

Section Two: Social Sciences

_____1. "The iron law of wages" is most closely
associated with the economic philosophy
of
(a) David Ricardo   (c) Adam Smith
(b) Leon Walrus   (d) Karl Marx

_____2. "Never give a sucker an even break" is
most closely associated with the economic philosophy of
(a) John D.   (c) William Claude
    Rockefeller   Dunkinfield
(b) J. P. Morgan   (d) J. Paul Getty

_____3. If the names of Joseph A. Schumpeter,
Wesley C. Mitchell and A. F. Burns were
mentioned in a discussion, the subject
matter under discussion would be most
likely that of
(a) money and   (c) housing
    banking   (d) social security
(b) business cycles

_____4. If the names Benson Fong, Mantan More-
land and Willie Best were mentioned in a
discussion, the subject matter under
discussion would be most likely
that of
(a) Race relations   (c) criminology
(b) rhythm and blues (d) the United
                          Nations

[98]

_____5. <u>Patterns</u> <u>of</u> <u>Culture</u> was written by
     (a) Margaret Mead   (c) Ashley Montagu
     (b) Ruth Benedict   (d) Bronislaw
                                    Malinowski

_____6. <u>Gamesmanship</u> was written by
     (a) Stephen Potter   (c) Eric Berne
     (b) Vince Lombardi   (d) Orestes Minoso

_____7. Which one of the following was most
     unlike the other three in his social and
     political outlook?
     (a) Robert Owen   (c) Louis Blanc
     (b) Mikhail Bakunin   (d) Charles Fourier

_____8. Which of the following was most unlike
     the other three?
     (a) Charlie Chaplin   (c) Oliver Hardy
     (b) Groucho Marx   (d) Lou Costello

_____9. The man who led Freedonia's struggle for
     freedom was
     (a) Giuseppe   (c) Simon Bolivar
         Garibaldi   (d) Leonid Kinsky
     (b) Groucho Marx

_____10. The man who led Germany's struggle for
     unification was
     (a) Kaiser   (c) Otto von
         Wilhelm II   Bismarck
     (b) Helmut von   (d) Helmut Dantine
         Moltke

_____11. The history teacher who wishes to make
     vivid the details of street life in
     18th century London would show students
     the work of
     (a) John Constable   (c) William Hogarth
     (b) Thomas   (d) Joshua Reynolds
         Gainsborough

_____12. The American West is best pictured in
the films of
(a) John Ford   (c) David Lean
(b) William Wyler   (d) Frank Capra

_____13. All of the following are correctly
paired with authors who wrote outstanding biographies about them, except
(a) Benjamin Franklin—Carl Van Doren
(b) Andrew Jackson—Marquis James
(c) Thomas Jefferson—Allan Nevins
(d) Abraham Lincoln—Carl Sandburg

_____14. All of the following are correctly
paired with actors who portrayed them
in films, except
(a) Andrew Jackson—Charlton Heston
(b) George A. Custer—Clark Gable
(c) Woodrow Wilson—Alexander Knox
(d) Abraham Lincoln—Raymond Massey

Section Three: Natural Sciences

_____1. Of the following phases of the moon, the
invisible one is called
(a) crescent   (c) new moon
(b) full moon   (d) waxing and
                         waning

_____2. Of the following phases of the moon, the
one that affects Lawrence Talbot the
most is
(a) crescent   (c) new moon
(b) full moon   (d) waxing and
                         waning

_____3. The time it takes for light from the sun
to reach the earth is approximately

(a) four years   (c) four months
(b) eight minutes   (d) sixteen years

___4. The number of tanna leaves needed to
keep the Mummy alive is
(a) seven   (c) three
(b) eleven   (d) nine

___5. The scientist who first synthesized DNA
was
(a) Kornberg   (c) Watson
(b) Sanger   (d) duVigneaud

___6. The actor who first played Dr. Franken-
stein (maker of men) in films was
(a) Boris Karloff   (c) Colin Clive
(b) Bela Lugosi   (d) Basil Rathbone

___7. Of the following radiation rays, the
ones which are the most resistant to
magnetic interference are
(a) alpha   (c) delta
(b) beta   (d) gamma

___8. Of the following, the one which causes
the most damage to Superman is
(a) Uranium   (c) Plutonium
(b) Kryptonite   (d) Lead

___9. Of the following, the one most involved
in the United States Space Program is
(a) James Goddard   (c) Werner von Braun
(b) Walter Cronkite (d) Edward Teller

___10. Of the following, the one most involved
in space flights to Vulcan is
(a) Buck Rogers   (c) Captain Video
(b) Flash Gordon   (d) Captain Midnight

THE RIGHT ANSWERS

<u>Scoring Instructions:</u> The testee shall be granted two (2) points for each of his answers which correspond with The Right Answers given below. Questions not answered—that is, left blank—shall neither receive nor lose credit. For each Wrong Answer—that is, an answer which does not correspond with The Right Answer—two (2) points shall be <u>deducted</u> from the testee's total score, as a penalty for guessing. Testees who can be trusted or intimidated <u>not</u> to change their answers may score their own papers (on the Honor System). Testees who cannot be so trusted or intimidated must submit their papers to another for scoring.

<u>Section One: Humanities</u>

1. B	14. B
2. C	15. C
3. D	16. A
4. B	17. D
5. B	18. B
6. C	19. C
7. D	20. A
8. B	21. C
9. A	22. B
10. C	23. C
11. C	24. B
12. A	25. D
13. B	

<u>Section Two: Social Sciences</u>

1. A	8. A
2. C	9. B
3. B	10. C
4. C	11. C
5. B	12. A
6. A	13. C
7. B	14. B

<u>Section Three: Natural Sciences</u>

1. C	6. C
2. B	7. D
3. B	8. B
4. C	9. C
5. A	10. B

Hey Bert, That Ain't No Eagle - It's a Hawk!

In July 1970, a really beautiful American, Kathy Huppe, eighteen, resigned her title as Miss Montana—and a chance to be a contestant in the Miss America Pageant—rather than keep her anti-war feelings to herself, as the pageant officials demanded.

Wouldn't it be nice if the next Miss America had Kathy's brains and patriotic spirit and would make some remarks like those Kathy was forced out for making—in her acceptance speech on network TV, with smiling Bert Parks humming in the background?

Now, wouldn't *that* be beautiful?

Starting a Student Publication:

⤙ TWO WAYS ⤚

I

In 1970, a student at one of New York City's high schools let it be known that he planned to publish an "underground" newspaper. The faculty grapevine had it "on good authority" that the paper would serve as an instrument for the expression of student dissatisfaction with current school policies. The student's plan made the principal and the staff uneasy, and a surprising number of faculty conference hours were devoted to discussions of his publication. Although they knew that final arrangements for the publication were vague, and actual production only a possibility, the teachers met to plan counterattacks and strategies designed to silence the student before he spoke. Some teachers argued that the publication ought to be suppressed entirely; others favored permitting its production but placing severe restrictions on its distribution. Two teachers proposed preparing an issue of the regular school newspaper which would rebut in advance any arguments a "radical" might be expected to publish. And one teacher argued quite convincingly for the application of what you would recognize—but he did not—as the judo principle. "If we try to block this newspaper with an obvious display of our power," he said, "we'll make a hero out of this kid and guarantee him support that he might not get if we just ignore him. If we act tolerant, and maybe even interested in his paper, we might take some of the wind out of his sails."

After extensive debate, the faculty settled on this compromise: They would allow publication and distribution of the paper, but it must be given away free of charge, and the student would have to write, edit, produce, and distribute it on his own—not school —time.

Shortly before the close of school for the summer holidays, the newspaper—a mimeographed issue—was in fact produced and distributed. The paper was in short supply (only two hundred copies were available to the five thousand students), but the four-page, one-column publication was greeted with a great deal of initial curiosity and interest by students and teachers alike. Among the teachers interest, curiosity, and apprehension quickly changed to relief and delight. There was nothing in the paper that threatened in the least the status quo within the school. Most of the articles dealt with problems over which schoolmasters have very little control—Vietnam, Cambodia, Kent State, Nixon, Mitchell, etc.— and these neither suggested nor demanded any action by the teachers or students. There were two or three paragraphs devoted to a generalized indictment of school procedures, but they offered no suggestions on what to change or how to go about it. The use of drugs was the subject of one short paragraph, whose main point seemed to be that since adults are inclined to booze, they have no right to criticize young people who experiment with pot or even harder stuff.

Among the students, curiosity and interest turned to vague disappointment, then to apathy. Their English teachers used the newspaper to point out the importance of grammar, spelling, and usage in effective communications. Their social studies teacher said he agreed—with most Americans—that Vietnam was tragic and Kent State shocking, and that, like them, he was impatient for such situations to end and personally powerless to do anything about them. The principal wrote a short note in the regular school newspaper, deploring many of the same school procedures the "underground" paper had criticized, but explaining that no one seemed to be able to come up with better ways to handle the administrative problems of running a large school. The phys ed teacher said he shared young people's contempt for alcoholic overindulgence among adults, but that the middle-class white view of the drug-user as a heroic freedom-seeker was too romantic for him—and for most of the poor and ghetto-trapped people who had been victimized by the hard narcotics economy. Less than a week after the first issue of the "underground" paper had appeared, the interest of the students had turned to anger—at its author. Their teachers took this response as evidence that most of the school's students were fairly content with the status quo and totally rejected the radical point of view. According to one teacher, the students "realized that school was a place to learn and that this sort of thing has no part in education." The teachers were wrong, of course. When the students were interviewed, a different picture emerged. They were angry, they said, because the "underground" editor hadn't bothered to work with other students, or to represent their views. As a result, he had misrepresented and trivialized what they thought the important issues were, so that they were easily dismissed by the teachers and administration. "This isn't the students' paper," said one boy. "It's just this guy's paper." "He tried to reform the world all by himself," said another, "and the rest of us have to suffer for it. We might really have got something going—now we all look like morons." Many of the students expressed the same point of view. They seemed to feel that the "underground" editor was showing off, pure and simple. And the "underground newspaper" turned out to be a one-shot affair.

II

When he learned that his high school principal regarded drug traffic as the number one problem in the school, a student decided to use this fact as the basis of a student movement. He spoke to his homeroom teacher, in confidence, telling him that he knew that the staff and many students were worried about the drug problem. Then he suggested that, if students and teachers worked together, a solution might be found. Finally, he asked for time during the homeroom period to discuss the problem with other students. The request was granted, partly because the teacher *was* worried, and partly because he did not object to being temporarily relieved of the daily problem of simultaneously taking roll and trying to keep thirty sophomores seated and quiet.

The student began the discussion the next morning by describing an incident—not very unusual—that had occurred in the cafeteria the previous day: some kids whom he had not recognized had roamed the lunchroom, selling a suspicious-looking powder.

He recalled another incident—also not unusual—earlier that day: Two boys had been cornered in the stairwell by four others, and were forced at knifepoint to empty their pockets. He suggested that the incidents were related, and asked for proposals for solving such problems. Some students, he found, were afraid to discuss the subject at all; they felt intimidated by the pushers, who might retaliate if there were a student move to upset their present position. Others were anxious not to incriminate their friends. Still others insisted that if the police and school officials were not able to deal with the drug traffic, teenagers were certainly less equipped to do the job. But a few students supported the assumption that they could help, and asserted that in some ways they were more expert to handle the problem than any of the adult authorities.

As the students talked, the homeroom teacher checked attendance and began to listen. He was surprised at the respect accorded to pushers, and was astonished that students would require courage to speak out against the spread of drugs. He also began to think, with some pleasure, that he might improve his own position in the school by using this discussion as an example, to his principal, of how to use homeroom periods more profitably. So when the students asked for additional time to continue their discussion the next day, he willingly agreed.

At the close of the third session, the students were satisfied that they had developed a reasonable working plan which they wanted to share with other students and faculty members. The homeroom teacher, delighted with his newly acquired self image as a man involved in student activity, volunteered to approach the principal with the plan. Some students objected to his interference, but others favored it on the grounds that a teacher could get further with a principal than could students. The group decided to take a chance and trust the teacher to present their plans. This is what they wanted:

1. To investigate strategies used in other schools to deal with drugs and drug-related problems.

2. To publish in prominent places around the school building the current laws—federal, state, and local—that restrict the sale and use of drugs.

3. To invite parents and members of the community to come to evening meetings to hear speakers and discuss the problem with them.

4. To ask teachers to volunteer to amend their current curriculum plans to include the study of drugs, and to see whether it would be possible to hold after-school sessions in which students and teachers would discuss the problem jointly. (This would provide a forum in which students and teachers might define their responsibilities to each other.)

5. To produce a student newspaper on drugs and other school problems.

6. To keep all discussions and reports given by students confidential, so as not to increase the fear some students felt about pusher retaliation.

The students agreed that these measures would not stop the use of drugs, nor would they cure any addicts. They did feel, however, that some potential users might avoid experimentation, and that some pushers might leave the school for places where resistance was less organized.

The principal was reluctant at first to say he would even consider the suggestions—especially item number five—but when the teacher pointed out that "the Board" would be impressed by the "innovative" idea of working with students on the drug problem, the principal agreed. After all, these were not "demands," but a chance to "experiment"; agreeing to the idea would improve his reputation in the community as a "forward-looking administrator" and a crusader against the evils of drugs.

At the next faculty meeting, the homeroom teacher introduced his star pupil, explaining that he represented students who were showing interest in the problem and a willingness to help to deal with it. The faculty agreed to try some of the suggestions. What else could it do? Two social studies teachers volunteered to explore the problem historically and socially. A science teacher suggested experimenting in his classes with the effects of drugs on mice. (His chairman vetoed the idea on the grounds that it would be difficult to keep track of the unused portions of the drugs used in the experiments.) A speech and drama teacher was willing to produce a play on the theme of drugs and drug abuse. A few

English teachers thought that a study of De Quincy, Coleridge, and other poets who admittedly used drugs might be worthwhile, but others thought that helping the students set up their publication might be more useful.

Thus, an aboveground "underground" newspaper was begun. Edited strictly by students, it was dedicated to the description of serious school problems and the proposal of solutions to them—beginning with drugs. But not ending there. The paper eventually dealt with the need for a student "Bill of Rights," an ombudsman to investigate student complaints, and greater student participation in designing the curriculum. As of this writing, the paper has become a regular feature of the school, and threatens to replace altogether the more conventional school newspaper, which has gone unread for years. Although some radical students still feel that, by definition, you can't have an "underground" paper if it's supported in any way by "the Establishment," the plain fact is that, in this school, changes are taking place that are a direct result of this publication. *And* serious inroads have in fact been made on the sale and use of drugs in the school.

MORAL: The Japanese have a saying that bamboo trees survive the ravages of a typhoon better than other trees because they bend with the wind instead of fighting it. No wonder that the Japanese invented judo.

Pike
and Minnows

Put some pike in a large tank of water. Put some minnows in the tank, too, but keep the pike and minnows separated by inserting a glass shield between them. The pike will naturally go for the minnows, since they dearly love to eat them. But they won't get them, because they will bump into the glass partition. The pike will keep trying—five times, ten times, maybe even fifty times. Then they will give up. When they give up, remove the glass partition. Now the minnows will swim freely among the pike—who are still very hungry. What happens next? The pike will not eat the minnows. Pike will even starve to death with all that food around them. Why? They have got it into their heads that they cannot get to the minnows. And even though the conditions which led to their original failure have been changed, the pike still can't get it into their heads that the minnows are now available.

There are a lot of people like pike. They get a slogan or sentence into their heads. The sentence becomes their reality. It may have been a "good" sentence at one time. But the times may change and make the sentence a "bad" one. Still, they can't get it out of their heads. And, in a way, they starve to death.

MORAL:
Examine your sentences.
The minnows may be all around you.

PARENT POWER

The young generation, . . . the articulate young rebels all around
the world who are lashing out against the controls to which they are
subjected, are like the first generation born into a new country.
They are at home in this time. Satellites are familiar in their skies.
They have never known a time when war did not threaten anni-
hilation. Those who use computers do not anthropomorphize
them; they know that they are programmed by human beings.
When they are given the facts, they can understand immediately
that continued pollution of the air and water and soil will soon
make the planet uninhabitable and that it will be impossible to
feed an indefinitely expanding world population. They can see
that control of conception is feasible and necessary. As members
of one species in an underdeveloped world community, they
recognize that invidious distinctions based on race and caste are
anachronisms. They insist on the vital necessity of some form of
world order. . . .

Once the fact of a deep, new, unprecedented world-wide generation gap is firmly established, in the minds of both the young
and the old, communication can be established again. But as long
as any adult thinks that he, like the parents and teachers of old,
can become introspective, invoke his own youth to understand
the youth before him, then he is lost.

MARGARET MEAD,
Culture and Commitment

For reasons Margaret Mead has explained brilliantly (above and
elsewhere), we are now experiencing an almost worldwide and
almost unbridgeable generation gap. This is not only unfortunate.
It is perverse. Precisely because the young and old see the world
differently, they need each other more than ever. The old need the

young, literally, as instructors in the "global village." The young need the old, because it is the old who still have the power. The problem is how to get them together.

Now, in this respect, the most important fact to keep in mind is that most parents not only love their children, but love them more than they love social institutions. They certainly love them more than they love the school curriculum, school regulations, teachers, professors, or anything else about the social system called education. This means that if students could persuade their parents that they are being harmed by school, their parents are more than likely to come to their assistance in fostering change.

The trouble is that students have been too busy establishing their image as "the first generation born in a new country." Some have taken every opportunity—through language or drugs or dress—to highlight their uniqueness and to alienate themselves from the world that their parents know. This is bad judo. It deprives the young of a major source of power in changing the system. If student power were allied with parent power, the results would be devastating, especially to conventional schooling procedures.

One of the earliest recorded examples of an alliance between students and parents against the system occurred in a Pennsylvania grammar school, circa 1795. The schoolmaster had adopted an infamous grammar book and was intent upon inflicting its lessons on the young. The students sought parental help. As quoted in *Old-time Schools and School-books*, "[each student] came to the master with the report that: 'Daddy says I needn't larn grammar. It's no use.'"

Of course, that's small stuff. But it was effective because all the ingredients of a smooth judo operation were present: The parents pay the schoolmaster to teach their children useful things. He who pays the piper calls the tune, right? Nobody denies that, not even the schoolmaster. The students understood this principle perfectly well, and so they went straight to the source of power. They probably also suspected that their parents were slightly suspicious of schoolmasters to begin with; and besides, they had an excellent issue. The study of grammar doesn't do anyone any good today, and it didn't in 1795, either. It wasn't all that tough, then, to turn the trick.

In today's world, things are a little more complex. Schools are bigger, and the influence of parents is not so direct. Still, there are many ways in which a student-parent alliance could work to turn some things around.

THE GRADING SYSTEM

Probably the most formidable obstacle to change in the schools is the grading system. Just about everyone who is part of a school knows this, including teachers. And yet no one seems to be able to get very far in disposing of grades. It is true that many teachers still *need* grades in order to keep their students in line—from elementary school through graduate school. It is also true that some parents think grades are needed in order for them to know how their children are doing. But even these people will concede that the purpose of an education has nothing to do with grades, and that grades tend to pollute the learning environment.

If you can persuade your parents that the grading system is harmful, that it is actually *depriving* you of an authentic education, then you may also be able to persuade them to initiate a lawsuit against the school system, in which they contend that:

1) A grade is a public document (which it is).

2) It is not the function of a school to make public evaluations of a student's behavior. (We are not talking here about professional schools.)

3) A bad grade constitutes a libelous statement, since it damages a student's reputation in his community, has the potential of restricting his future opportunities, and adversely affects his future earnings.

4) A permanent injunction should be issued against the school to prevent it from making known, in any form, the results of student performance to anyone except the student and his parents.

If you have a younger brother or sister who is an elementary school student, the suit would best be advanced in his or her name, since there really is no justification whatsoever for grading elementary school children. A similar suit, however, should also be initiated in behalf of high school and college students.

Schools would contend that evaluation is a necessary phase of the learning process. The reply: Perhaps. But why must an evaluation be recorded and, therefore, be made public? Schools would contend that other schools, higher in the system, need to have a record of a student's past performance. The reply: For what reason? Let colleges and graduate schools invent ways to determine which students should or shouldn't be admitted. It is not the business of a lower school to assist in this process. The same reply would be applicable to the argument that industry needs to know what someone's school record has been. Let industry solve the problem of who is acceptable to it. The schools have no business being implicated in the decision.

Incidentally, it should be relatively easy to prove that bad grades not only hurt a student's economic future, but threaten his psychological well-being as well. That is, his capacity for successful learning in the future is damaged by a poor grade. It will be contended by schools that although grades may penalize certain students, the grades are administered impartially on the basis of objective standards of performance. It will not be difficult to show that grades are entirely subjective; that even when they are based on short-answer tests, the tests themselves are subjective; and that the personality of a teacher is the main factor in determining the grade given to a particular student.

Even if such a lawsuit as this produces no salutary result (or if you can find no one to undertake the expense of pursuing it), it would be worthwhile to enlist the support of parents in making the grading system a public issue, anyway. The points made above can be pressed at PTA meetings and other forums. Parents might insist that no grades be given their children unless teachers are also evaluated, and the results of *their* evaluations are made public. If *that* point were won—no student grades without teacher grades—you might see a swift and decisive end to the grading system.

It is essential that students and parents be together on this issue. This means that students will have to work to persuade their parents that something important is at stake here. If they can, then we can practically guarantee some results. Schools can withstand student power. They can withstand parent power. They cannot withstand both.

One final point: At the very least, you ought to persuade your parents to make known their views on grades to your teachers. There are many teachers who would gladly abandon conventional grading if they had any kind of support from parents.

TEXTBOOKS

Almost any school administrator can testify to the power of parent pressure in the matter of textbook selection. The trouble is that almost all such pressure has come from conservatives. When "liberal" parents have been involved at all, their role has been largely to defend the status quo. But why? There is almost nothing defensible about school textbooks, and except for some cro-magnons of the Birch Society, the conservatives are right in their basic assumption: Textbooks *are* biased. Moreover, they are biased in a way that the conservatives either haven't noticed or don't much care about. Textbooks assume that all students are more or less alike; that students learn in the same way; and that students are interested in the same things. For these reasons, the textbook is responsible, perhaps more than any other single factor, for the rigidity of school curricula. If we can rid ourselves of textbooks, we will open the way to some really creative changes in the curriculum.

What is really needed, then, is a concerted effort by students and parents to challenge the use of standardized and standardizing texts. But it is essential that this not be accomplished in the familiar mindless, right-wing manner. We require serious critiques of current texts, critiques that demonstrate the *intellectual biases* of texts, not their political biases. (It is true that almost all texts are politically biased, but their biases are so bland that very few students can be effectively propagandized by them.) It can be shown that texts try to teach that there is a single, right answer to almost every question; that obedience to authority is of the utmost importance; that the lessons of the past are invariably applicable to the future; that all students should think about problems in the same way; that question-asking is not very important; and that answer-giving and, in particular, memorizing, are the preeminent intellectual skills. In our opinion, these are the biases that most need to be eliminated.

If students can explain to their parents how these biases work to stifle intellectual excellence, if students can give evidence of their presence in texts, then parental pressure could be decisive in eliminating required textbooks. Here's why:

1) Most teachers do not have great confidence in texts, anyway. They use them because *someone else* usually requires that they do.

2) The someone else is usually a supervisor or department chairman who believes that the use of texts will promote conformity in the curriculum, but who rarely can defend the text on *intellectual* grounds.

3) Textbooks are costly, and everyone would save money if they were eliminated.

4) The rate at which the "facts" in any subject area are changing today is far greater than the rate at which textbooks wear out and can be replaced with updated versions. As a result, much of the information in any set of school texts is obsolete by the time students "learn" it. This means, among other things, that students will have to waste a substantial portion of their education careers in *unlearning* the inaccurate information and perceptions they learned earlier.

In other words, the use of textbooks is mostly ritualistic: The practice lingers on long after the purpose has been lost. If there is responsible, serious, and informed criticism of the practice, and if it comes from both parents and students, the argument should be effective.

Here is a list of questions that might help you in evaluating texts:

1) Is the learner asked closed or open-ended questions?

2) What kinds of "answers" does the text require?

3) Do the questions asked of the learner seem important? To whom? The learner? The teacher?

4) Is the learner given a great many things to do? What kinds of things?

5) Does he have choices? Are they realistic ones?

6) Is the learner given a *variety* of things to do?

7) Does the text seem to assume that all learners are the "same"?

8) Does the text assume that students learn from each other?

9) Does the text offer the learner novel things to do?

10) Does the text propose most of the assignments?

11) Does it give students any opportunity to propose assignments?

12) Does the text encourage students to challenge its own statements?

13) Does the text state anywhere what its particular biases are or what its general point of view is?

14) Does the text indicate that there are other points of view on, different approaches to, and different methods of studying the field it has taken as its subject?

15) Are students required to share the same opinion on any subject?

16) In what ways does the text restrict the students' interests?

17) In what ways does the text expand the students' interests?

18) What is the copyright date on the text?

19) What is the most recent date mentioned in the text?

20) How often does the text use words and expressions like "Always," "Never," "Invariably," "Everyone," "No one," "All authorities agree," and the like?

TEACHERS' SALARIES

In most jobs, if a man does not do what he is paid to do, he is considered a failure. In teaching, when that happens, the *student* is considered a failure. This is a point around which a good deal of parental support can be marshaled. Why should teachers be immune from the ordinary reward and punishment system most people must contend with? Your parents must contend with "merit ratings" on *their* jobs, so it should not be difficult to persuade them that teachers ought to as well.

One strong point you will want to make in this context is that the only sane definition of "teach" is "to enable another to learn." The tests a teacher gives constitute a very specific definition—and remember, it is the teacher's *own* definition—of what he or she is trying to enable students to learn. When a student fails the test, it can only mean that the *teacher* failed to teach him what he or she set out to teach. If the "class average" is 75 per cent, then the teacher's performance was only 75 per cent effective. This fact might provide the basis for a *dynamite* parent-student proposal: A teacher should be paid only that percentage of his or her salary that corresponds to the "class average" on the tests he or she gave over the year. Such a proposal, if accepted by the school system, would probably have one of two effects: Either the grading system would vanish overnight, or almost all students would find themselves with "averages" of between 90 and 100 per cent. And if the proposal were rejected, it would increase parent-student power by exposing to the community at large the utter fraud that schools and teachers are.

Apart from this, it will be no simple matter to invent a merit system that would actually work to the students' advantage—that is, a system that would help reduce the number of incompetents in the school. But whatever you come up with, it ought to include opportunities for both parents and students to evaluate the performance of teachers.

A STUDENT UNION AND THE LAW

If a student union were organized, not along the lines of a cafeteria with a ping pong table at one end but along the lines of a labor union, there's no reason why legal counsel could not be retained to institute legal proceedings on behalf of student interests as circumstances warranted.

As the Supreme Court has said, there is nothing anywhere that says students give up their rights as American citizens just because they are enrolled in one school or another. *Every* incursion upon a student's civil rights as a citizen of the United States can be brought to a court of law for adjudication. Experience to date indicates quite sharply that the law supports the rights of students, whether it has to do with the length of hair or the style of clothes, much more frequently than it does the authority of the school. And of course the whole area of invasion of privacy in the form of school record-keeping is wide open for legal testing and interpretation.

The time is right for the educational equivalent of Ralph Nader to emerge, with schools—rather than monster corporations—as the litigants in test cases.

Student power in the form of a union would make the power of the law available to students. But it is simply a fact of the system that justice is available mostly to those with the power to pay for it. Therefore you would need your parents' help in order to get started. Many parents are themselves members of labor unions, and it would be strange if you could not enlist their support for a student union. But remember, labor unions aren't what they used to be—namely, radical organizations. Most union-minded people don't want to overthrow the system. In seeking parental support, you will probably need to show that the purpose of your union is the same as the purpose of your parents' union: To give protection to its members and to improve their situation.

In all the efforts you make toward obtaining parent power, you will need to get the truth about how your school operates and what goes on in it out to where the public at large can get at it. Underground newspapers are great for getting the word to other students, but for getting together with members of the establishment—that is, parents—they're just about useless. If you try, you can probably get space in the local newspaper—not just to air your opinions, but to print copies of stuff that comes out in the school, like administrative memos, rules and regulations, and so on. And you can probably get air time, at least on local radio stations, and maybe even on local TV stations. You can always get a hearing at community meetings like those held by the PTA, civic and business organizations, and church groups. If you try.

It is best to have the burden of the truth you are trying to communicate rest on authentic, verifiable statements, actions, and events that occurred within the school. If you make this truth available, you won't need to lay your opinion on anybody. They'll form the same opinion if you give them the data they need. Many of them will, anyway. For example, think of the impact it would have on people if students made tape recordings of what goes on in school, then played the recordings at public meetings or on local radio programs. Nothing elaborate—just recordings of what is said by teachers in classes or by administrators over the p.a. system in secondary schools. (College memos could be read onto the tape and copies could be made for anyone interested in having such curious documents.) Hardly anything could (or would need to be) added if you played a real recording of how it is. And if anyone objects to your making such recordings, tell them that the FBI does it all the time, so it must be OK.

© 1970 CHICAGO SUN-TIMES

All the World's a Stage--
And an Echo Chamber

In *Only You, Dick Darling*, Merle Miller recounts an episode in his life that may not seem to you to make any sense at all, but we like it, so here it is:

He was having a great deal of difficulty at one point in his life; nothing seemed to be going right. So he went back to the little town he was born and grew up in, sort of trying to get a perspective on what was happening. There was an old lady in the town (she may have been a relative), and she spoke with an accent. He had a deep affection for her and had regarded her as a good source of advice in his youth, so on this occasion he sought her out to get her advice again.

After recounting his trials and tribulations to her, he waited for her to respond. She thought for a while and then she said, and it was all she said, "Yoost remember dat de yoohoo dat you yoohoo is de yoohoo dat comes back to you."

"We Has Met the Enemy and He Is Us."

POGO

In *The Human Use of Human Beings,* Norbert Wiener points out many distinctions among different ways of looking at and thinking about things. One such distinction is particularly relevant for soft revolutionaries. It can make the difference between being submerged in self-exhausting and self-defeating strategies and being free enough to work effectively for much-needed change. It can also help you to distinguish between the symptoms and the causes of problems, and so save you a great deal of time and energy that you might otherwise waste in fighting a nonexistent enemy. What we are referring to is Wiener's distinction between a "Manichean" and an "Augustinian" way of viewing the way things happen. The Manichean way can be called "primitive," and the Augustinian "scientific."

The Manichean man views "evil" (anything that frustrates or bothers or scares him) as the result of a conscious, deliberate plot by an ingenious agent who is his enemy, and whose primary purpose for being is to screw him. This tendency to personify and personalize natural phenomena, as well as human failings, is one of the most ubiquitous human characteristics, especially among pre-scientific people—including most Americans in the second decade of the nuclear-space age.

The "devil" is perhaps the basic Manichean metaphor. He-She-It serves several self-defeating functions, not the least of which is that of shifting the responsibility for some mess from oneself to "someone" else. Flip Wilson's routine about "the devil made me do it" makes the self-delusion in this kind of thinking highly visi-

[123]

ble; and the recognition of our tendency to think this way is what makes his routine so funny.

Today in America, after more than twenty years of indoctrination, many of our institutions and citizens are so paranoid about "communists" and "communism" that about the only response they have to anything they see as a problem—from pollution to integration to Vietnam—is to call it part of a "communist plot." This absolves them of any responsibility for causing the problem in the first place, and insures that they will *not* engage in any behavior that is responsive to the problem. "Communists" serve about the same function today that "the Devil" did in the Middle Ages. So do "hippies," "militants," and "campus radicals," which is why Agnew has become so popular.

Those who operate from the Manichean perspective may "get busy" and put lots of energy and resources into fighting "the enemy," but because their basic metaphor confines them to hollering at symptoms, they scarcely ever get to dealing with the causes of a problem. The result is that the more activity they engage in, the worse the problem gets. The Pentagon and the State Department (which may mean the CIA) are probably the most expensive examples at the moment of this kind of self-destroying thought. The more men and material they devote to "solving" the Vietnam problem, the worse things get.

Not the least of the burdens of a Manichean view of things is that while all the attention and energy are devoted to doing dumb things, there is little or no chance for anybody to do anything smart.

The Augustinian view is essentially the one stated by Pogo: We has met the enemy and he is us. Or as Einstein said: "I cannot believe that God plays dice with the world." Wiener puts it this way: the Augustinian opponent is not a power in itself, but the measure of our own weakness. We can deal with "it" because it is not perverse or malicious. "It" is our frustrations, our lack of understanding, and our failures; and it exists always to the extent that we do not have a realistic view of how things are. Which means that the Augustinian devil can be exorcised or defeated by intelligence.

In the Augustinian view of the universe, for example, one considers chaos more probable than order, *not* as the result of any activity on the part of a wily and evil opponent, but just because that's the way it is. Scientists, like Wiener, call this universal tendency toward "disorder" *entropy*. Apparently the process of the universe, from galaxies through stars and right down to the atom, is one of cosmic equilibrium-seeking. All the little positives are gravitating toward all the little negatives, and when they finally meet up, there is complete equilibrium—which means, for humans, death. Life then is an enclave of temporary anti-entropic activity—organized disequilibrium, or pockets of directed energy. All forms of "order" are anti-entropic, and this includes all forms of organized human behavior. And human organization has only *one* basic tool to use in combatting entropy: Wiener calls it *information*. By *information* he means "what is exchanged with the outer world as we adjust to it, and make our adjustments felt upon it." The process of receiving and using information is the process of our adjusting to the contingencies of the outer environment, and of our living effectively within that environment. *To live effectively is to live with adequate information.*

Our point is, of course, that it is the Augustinian view, not the Manichean, which provides the most realistic perspective from which to see and act upon problems in the schools. The Manichean view of schools insures failure because it invents a pseudo-enemy ("the Establishment") and depends upon slogans and clichés rather than information.

To take an example: There is a radical school publication called *The Teacher Paper* (280 North Pacific, Monmouth, Oregon). The young couple who put it together are serious people of good intentions. Last year, they published *The Guerrilla Manual*, an elongated, one-page list of 162 suggestions for tactics to be used by those who are concerned with "humanizing" the schools. Some of the suggestions are very good indeed, and for that reason you might want to send for a copy. But because so much of the perspective of its authors is Manichean, many of the tactics are self-destructive. The manual is aimed at teachers who would like to change the system, and includes the advice to place mousetraps in lockers on locker-check day, to publish bogus memos, to walk on the grass wherever there are "Don't Walk On The Grass" signs, to place Saran wrap over waste-cans and teachers' mailboxes, to put silly putty in the office ditto machine, and to pour limburger

[125]

cheese in the confidential file. Of course, this is just silliness, but behind the silliness lurks the Manichean devil: the assumption that your "opponent" is evil, is out to destroy you, is somehow larger than human and thereby somewhat less than human, and on that account you are warranted to use all the obnoxious "tactics" that a fertile and outraged imagination can conceive. It is significant that the final suggestion of *The Guerrilla Manual* is a slogan: Up With People! As you would expect, about half of the suggestions involve doing things that would make many people miserable. Apparently "Up With People" means "Up With Our People, And Screw The Other People."

The Augustinian view is one that is reality-oriented, not slogan-oriented, and it usually produces action that is relevant to the problem being dealt with because it is based on the acquisition and use of information, and it includes a continuing assessment of the feedback that results from the use of that information. It is, in short, oriented to the actualities of the outside environment, where the Manichean is oriented to "devils" that exist only metaphorically in a rhetoric that mirrors only the paranoid-schizophrenia of those who use and are used by it.

Examples of the Augustinian perspective can be found, in fact, right in *The Guerrilla Manual*. They include the advice to teachers to invite parents to class frequently, to meet with college faculties to inform them about what's happening in the schools, to organize a classroom teachers' association, and to produce a teachers' newsletter. These tactics *increase* the flow of information, which, in turn, provides the basis for informed decisions. The result is to keep entropy under control, where it belongs. These tactics also address themselves to problems (like the need for more teacher power), and not to symptoms (like the excessive number of memos). These tactics also tend to move people together, not pull them apart.

The language of the Manichean perspective practically insures that people *will* be pulled apart. "If you were *not with us,* you were *against us.*" That's one of Jerry Rubin's lines from *Do It!*

> That's what Hitler said.
> That's what Joe McCarthy said.
> That's what rednecks say.

That's what super-blacks say.
That's what Agnew says.

"It's better to be dead than _____." That's a Manichean talking, no matter what he puts in the blank. That's the language of the Weathermen or the Minutemen or the Panthers or the U.S. Marine Corps or some other group of crazies on some Thanatos Express. What being dead can accomplish is not clear to us. Death is the triumph of entropy.

One final point. The Augustinian view is not by any means morally neutral. From its perspective, there are many different ways to distinguish between "good" and "bad." The way we do it is simple, or rather, simple-seeming. We use what we call a "pragmatic" approach. Our version of pragmatism holds that you judge whether something is "good" or "bad" on the basis of the difference it makes. If something makes a difference in the direction of helping human beings, then it's "good." If it makes a difference in the direction of harming human beings, then it's "bad." If something makes no difference, then we judge it to be dumb, because it takes time and energy away from doing something that could make a difference that helps.

That's just the beginning, though, since one quickly discovers that what may be good for some people may not be good for others. But being dead isn't good for anyone, and neither is pouring limburger cheese in confidential files.

Antidisestablishmentarianism

Establishmentarianism is the Manichean belief that all the particular and general woes of the world were created and are perpetuated by The Establishment.

Disestablishmentarianism is the Manichean belief that all the particular and general woes of the world would disappear if we could just destroy The Establishment.

Antidisestablishmentarianism is the Augustinian perspective of the soft revolutionary. It includes the beliefs that

> *the establishment is only a metaphor for*
> *   organized power;*
> *it is individual people who wield that power;*
> *individual people are changeable and*
> *   accessible to reason,*
> *especially when reason and change can be shown*
> *   to be in their self-interest;*
> *among people of influence there are many untapped*
> *   sensitivities and repositories of good will;*
> *everybody is somebody else's establishment*
> *   (in some context or other);*
> *which means that*
> *more often than we think,*
> *when we denounce establishments,*
> *we are denouncing ourselves.*

SATURDAY REVIEW, MARCH 15, 1969

"No! Please . . . I'm relevant, I tell you . . . relevant! . . ."

JUDO
IN THE SECRET SOCIETY

In June of 1970, an audible minority of college students elected to Phi Beta Kappa declined to become members. Some who accepted used the opportunity for soft revolutionary purposes.

Carol Matzkin, a senior at Berkeley, said, "I don't know how to spell, or how many quarts there are in a gallon. All I know is how to get around in the system." Perhaps to illustrate her last point, she accepted election to PBK, but said that she did so with "shame and guilt" because she thinks society and the system she knows how to beat are "rotten and degenerate."

At the College of William and Mary in Virginia, where Phi Beta Kappa was founded as a secret society in 1776, one new member seized the opportunity of his election to denounce the society in the same room where its first meeting was held during the Revolutionary War.

Apparently, Phi Beta Kappa is being made to discover that it is facing the same basic questions that most of the institutions and organizations of American society are facing—particularly the question as to how judgments are made in a time of great and rapid change.

The elimination of Phi Beta Kappa as it presently exists may not be the highest item on the soft revolutionary's agenda, but it should be on it, and may be one of the easier projects to accomplish. If you're a member, resign. Take as many with you as possible. If you're asked to join, (a) decline, or (b) accept and then denounce the organization.

If you're in high school, the same thing goes for the National Honor Society.

ON DEFINING

When the New York Thruway Authority faced the problem of an excessive number of speed limit violations, it invented a solution that makes so much sense that the guy who came up with the idea was probably fired.

They raised the speed limit.

In France, during the summer of 1970, there were some similar problems with "moving violations" by motorists. Here was the solution:

When a motorist was seen violating a traffic regulation, rather than being overtaken by a swaggering cop who snarled the French equivalent of "Where's the fire?", he would be overtaken by a sports car and waved to a stop by an exceptionally attractive young woman, who would then approach him bearing a bouquet of flowers. She would present the bouquet to him, kiss him the way a seriously interested woman would, and then ask him to please be more careful in his driving.

There was no information available to us as to what happened if the driver was a woman, but we'd guess that the policemen selected for this assignment were chosen because their characteristics complemented the function to be fulfilled.

(Yes, it has occurred to us that this procedure might serve to induce more traffic violations than it prevents, but that may be because we think like Americans rather than like Frenchmen.)

At a prep school in New York State, one of the annual activities consisted of the theft of a pair of the headmaster's drawers, which were then run up the flagpole on top of a steeple by the boy who stole them. The first boy to do this became the official school hero for the year.

Recognizing that such rites of passage are important to a boy's definition of himself, the headmaster didn't want to stop the activity. But because of the precarious position of the flagpole (it was on top of a seventy-foot-high steeple covered with a slippery slate roof and bordered by a concrete-covered courtyard), he was really worried that some boy would slip and fall. He didn't want that to happen.

His problem, then, was to get the boys to abandon the steeple-climbing. He knew that threats and punishment would only serve to increase the value of the event, so he tried to think of some way to *devalue* it so that it would no longer have the significance necessary for the boys to persist in it. Here was his solution: He put up a ladder so that any kid, even the dumbest lump in school, could climb up the steeple anytime he wanted to. When anybody could do it anytime, it lost its value. Like Thoreau said, "What is too easily achieved is too lightly esteemed."

At a junior high school in New York City, the teachers had a great deal of trouble keeping their students inside the classrooms. To be specific, many students would wander through the hallways during classtime. Sometimes, they would run and fight and scream, which on occasion was dangerous—and always distracting to those inside the classrooms. The "wanderers" were threatened many times, but to no avail. An assistant principal, in an unprecedented attack of the smarts, came up with this solution: She announced that the school was instituting a radical educational plan, known as "The Open Hall Policy." The plan made staying in the halls a legitimate educational activity, as long as running, screaming, and fighting were confined to specific corridors. As a consequence, a lot of kids stopped wandering in the halls—and those who stayed there usually talked quietly among themselves.

Our last information was that principals from other schools were visiting this one to observe "The Open Hall Policy" in action.

As a method for solving problems, these cases have something in common. In each instance, the problem was solved by *redefining* the meaning of a word or an event. In the first case, the definition of "speeding" was changed. In the second case, the definition of how "bad" a moving violation is was changed. In the third and fourth, an "unauthorized" school activity was redefined as an "authorized" one.

Now, this process is a very powerful instrument for positive change, if used with imagination and intelligence. Consider how much criminal activity could be eliminated simply by redefining certain "criminal" acts as "legal" ones. In New York State, abortion has been so redefined. Perhaps in the near future smoking pot will be defined as legal, drug addiction will be defined as a medical matter, and prostitution defined as a "major weapon against sex crimes." If that happened, our society would have eliminated about 50 per cent of all "criminal" activity in the country, *merely by changing the meaning of words*. This would be an example of using the judo approach against the Newspeak tendencies in our society.

We have already become accustomed to the redefinitions of words by the Pentagon and other government agencies—the most terrifying example being the remark of a major in Vietnam who said that we had to destroy a town in order to save it. But the point is that redefining words cuts both ways. New definitions can be used to shut off perceptions, to dry up feelings, to make the unacceptable acceptable. But they can also open people to new perceptions, intensify their feelings, and help make them more aware of their responsibilities. Why give the Nixons, Agnews, and Mitchells a monopoly on the defining process?

In the context of school reform, there is a suggestion elsewhere in this book that we can triple the number of teachers in any school system by redefining who is qualified to be a teacher. Here are some other possibilities:

If students were urged to cooperate fully with each other when taking tests, everyone would benefit and "cheating" would be eliminated.

If compulsory attendance were eliminated, there would be no "truants."

If "student failure" were defined as "teacher failure" (as suggested elsewhere in the book), we would eliminate student failure, and probably incompetent teachers. In fact, Albert Shanker, President of the UFT, inadvertently revealed this when, in opposing a plan for contract teaching—no results, no pay—he said that in such a situation, teachers would probably give students the answers. Well, why not? That's what teachers are supposed to do in the present system, isn't it?

Suppose "a good student" were defined as one who can ask useful questions, instead of as one who can parrot textbooks and teachers?

If we stopped thinking of "school" as a *place,* and started thinking of it as a series of problems, what would happen?

What would happen if there were no "schools" at all? How would youth conduct their "education"?

What would happen if we abandoned the notion that elders are well suited to "instruct" the young?

What would happen if all the "extracurricular" activities were redefined as "major" subjects, and all major subjects were made extracurricular activities?

What would happen if we assumed that "instruction" or teaching of any systematic kind was harmful to the learner?

What would happen if "education" were solely concerned with what we presently call "emotional development"?

What would happen if students had complete freedom to select their own teachers?

If all university credentials disappeared, on what basis would you define a "teacher"? or a "physician"? or anything else?

All of these questions have to do with the way we define things, and the possibilities in redefining them. Give it some thought. Meanwhile,

Read the "fable" of the six blind men and the elephant.
Read the accounts—about anything—by six different "experts."
Read or see *Rashomon.*
Read the testimony of six "eyewitnesses" to any event.
Read accounts of judicial decisions from different parts of the United States over the past hundred years as to the meaning of the Constitution.
Read the legal definition of what a "Negro" "is" in each of the Southern states.
Read about what's going on in Israel with respect to determining who is and who is not "a Jew."

THE STUDENTS
and
THE HARD-HATS

One of the basic assumptions of the soft revolution—and one of the strongest weapons of those who participate in it—is the idea that, although two people may have vast *ideological* differences, they will always share a large number of interests and beliefs. For example, we know two men who have never agreed, so far as we know, on *any* political issue of the past fifteen years. And yet they both have the same taste in clothing, in movies, in novels, in entertainment, in women, in manners, in food, and in cars. They don't talk much about these common tastes, because when they are together they mostly like to insult each other for holding stupid political opinions. It's never much mattered, since they have had no need to work together for a mutually satisfying goal. But if they did, it would be awfully important to them to acknowledge how many opinions they do share.

Here is a case where exactly that idea was used by some students:

In late spring of 1970, construction workers in the Wall Street section of New York City attacked some college students, presumably because the latter held improper political opinions. There developed from this an almost instant, and thoroughly violent, polarization of students and hard-hats throughout the city. Some people did not view this as a "problem"—except, perhaps, for the police—but others did, particularly ten undergraduates at a municipal college. They decided to do something.

Now, it so happened that there was much construction work in progress on their own campus, which meant that there were hard-hats all around. The students thought it would be important if non-violent communication lines between them and the hard-hats could be opened. So they bought three six-packs of Schaefer beer and, at lunch time, approached the largest construction site on campus. They sent a particularly naive professor ahead to make the initial contact, since they had no guarantee that the construction workers wouldn't be inclined to a very fast draw. The professor came within twenty-five yards of the foreman and, with the beer held in front of him, indicated that he and the students had come to sign a peace treaty. The foreman was bemused, and signaled the professor to advance and explain himself—which he did. He said it was bad business when two groups of people are fighting with each other, and that perhaps it was possible for students and workers to get to know something more about each other than their political opinions. The beer, he explained, was a peace offering which the students wished to share with the workers. The foreman could not resist, and helped to round up six or seven of his men. And so their discussions began, and lasted for two weeks—every day at lunch time. During the second week, the hard-hats sprung for the beer (although one of the things the students learned was that not all hard-hats drink beer).

Now, what was on everyone's mind was Cambodia, Vietnam, Kent State, and the American flag. But that is not what they talked about. At first. They talked about air pollution, congested streets, inadequate garbage collection, inflation, the generation gap, and other subjects on which there was bound to be agreement. This gave everyone a chance to get to know the others, and even to like one another. When people like one another, or when they discover that *they agree about many things,* they find it easier to talk without anger about subjects on which they disagree. This the students and workers did. Except in two cases, they did not change one another's minds on Vietnam or Cambodia. There was, however, much exchanging of sources of information. One of the students commented that "a major difference between us is that *they* get their prejudices from the *Daily News,* and we get *ours* from *The New York Times.*"

Nonetheless, something important *did* happen. Although they did not change one another's minds about particular political issues, they changed one another's minds about *each other,* and this in itself was such an extraordinary event that NBC prepared a television documentary on what happened. The documentary was presented on NBC's *First Tuesday,* and one worker asked after seeing it, "Why don't you ever see people *talking* on TV, the way we were?"

One of the students made the following comment about the experience: "Mainly, what I learned was that someone can be with you *and* against you at the same time. Or maybe I mean that you can be *with* someone but against a few of his opinions."

Nader's Raiders

Ralph Nader is one of America's most effective soft revolutionaries. His basic strategy is, of course, judo. For example, since one of America's favorite maxims is that we are a country of laws, not men, he uses the courts continually to call attention to the ways in which powerful corporate interests hustle consumers. Most of his staff are lawyers, which means that they know how corporation lawyers operate to make it easier for their clients to cheat the public. That Nader has been effective is beyond question. Automobile manufacturing corporations have been forced to call back hundreds of thousands of cars over the past few years in order to correct badly constructed mechanisms. Nader himself was secretly "investigated" by General Motors, which hoped it could use certain private facts of his life to force him to desist. Nader used the courts in that situation too, and forced GM to pay for its villainy.

But his greatest contribution yet may be in the field of education, for Nader's *idea* is more important than even the sensational revelations of his staff. His idea is this: As America has increased in organizational and technological complexity, the only way the public can be kept informed about what's going on is by having dedicated young professionals doing systematic research into problem areas. Nader's particular group is popularly known as Nader's Raiders, and their main concern is consumer protection. But has it occurred to anyone that there are hundreds of thousands of other "dedicated young professionals" who are ready and willing to carry on such work in other areas? They are called graduate students. At present they are mainly being kept under wraps by a system of training that is completely obsolete, irresponsible, and, to say the least, unloved by those who must participate in it. Graduate students spend their time sitting in classrooms; writing term papers no one besides the professor will ever read, or care to; and trying to overcome obstacles that often have little or no meaning to them—for example, foreign language exams, statistics courses, orals, and, hovering above all, that monument to to the triumph of irrelevance, the doctoral dissertation.

Suppose we could somehow mobilize the talent and energy of graduate students to provide our nation's first line of defense against ignorance and charlatanism. Suppose there were counterparts to Nader's Raiders in every university in the country—students whose graduate training consisted of doing systematic investigations into public problems and of communicating the results to the widest possible audience. Suppose this could be done even in one university. What would it be like?

In point of fact, such a program is being contemplated at one university. Here is a description of the program, as taken from the prospectus for it. (Local catalogues please copy.)

A Prospectus for a Ph.D. Program in Media Ecology

Media ecology is the study of transactions among people, their messages, and their message systems. More particularly, media ecology studies how media of communication affect human perception, feeling, understanding, and value; and how our interaction with media facilitates or impedes our chances of survival. The word *ecology* implies the study of environments—their structure, content, and impact on people. An environment is, after all, a complex message system which regulates ways of feeling and behaving. It structures what we can see and say and, therefore, do. Sometimes, as in the case of a courtroom, or classroom, or business office, the specifications of the environment are explicit and formal. In the case of media environments (e.g., books, radio, film, television, etc.), the specifications are more often implicit and informal, half-concealed by our assumption that we are dealing with machines and nothing more. Media ecology tries to make these specifications explicit. It tries to find out what roles media force us to play, how media structure what we are seeing, why media make us feel and act as we do. Media ecology is the study of communications technology as environments.

This document proposes a "course of study" in media ecology.

The best way to describe the program is to describe what the students will in fact *do* and what outcomes are expected. Their activities will be divided among four areas: Media History, Media Literacy and Creativity, Media Research, and Media Perspectives and Criticism.

MEDIA HISTORY

Each student will be required to study the history of technology and communication, as well as "inquire into" the *future* of both. This activity will take the form of three "courses" (the only "courses" the students will "take"). Two of the courses will deal exclusively with media history—that is, the social, political, aesthetic, and economic effects of past media and media innovation. The third course will be in futurology—the study of the social, political, aesthetic, and economic effects of future media and media change. No grades will be given in the courses. The student will be evaluated by writing a monograph which attempts to solve a particular problem dealing with the future. He may, for example, select some general theme such as the future of educational systems, the future of air travel, the future of medical care, the future of architecture, the future of representative government, the future of religious systems, etc. His monograph would then identify a problem or problems that the future will impose in this area, and offer a design for solving the problem. The purpose of the monograph is twofold: To have the student demonstrate an ability to *do* something with his historical knowledge, and to form a library of futuristic, scholarly, problem-solving literature that would be valuable to the national and world community.

MEDIA LITERACY AND CREATIVITY

Each student will be required to work toward the acquisition of "multi-media literacy." We are *not* training technicians, but it is reasonable to expect that each of our graduates will have a minimal degree of competence in the use of various twentieth century (and possibly twenty-first century) media. These would include, for example, computers, motion pictures, television, tape recorders, radio, photography, etc. The intention here is to have the student learn some of the important technical problems of several media, so that he may have an understanding of their creative capabilities and limitations. Indeed, if the medium is the message (or, if the medium is even *sometimes* the message), our students will need to know, in practical terms, something about the structure of various media. The best way to learn this is to work with, to produce something in a medium. Thus, students will be expected to spend some considerable amount of time in the media lab, and will eventually have their skills and understanding evaluated by producing at least two creative works—for example, a radio broadcast, a film, a computer program, a photographic exhibit, a television tape, etc.

Included in "media literacy" must be a consideration of the problems of interpersonal communication: its structure, its effects, its limitations, its creative possibilities. In other words, in personal terms, one's language as well as one's body and entire metamessage mechanism are media of utmost importance. The psychology of interpersonal communication will be included in the program by requiring each student to be involved in at least one T-group experience. The purpose of such an experience is twofold: first, to offer the student an opportunity to learn about, modify, and extend his own repertoire of communication techniques (verbal and nonverbal), and, second, to provide students with a laboratory for the study of interpersonal communication. Thus, in conjunction with the T-group experience, a seminar will be conducted to stimulate extensive discussions of the psychology of human communication.

MEDIA RESEARCH

Each student will be required to conduct three studies during his program. One of these must be part of a "team" research effort, the other two to be individual efforts. The general model for such studies (that is, for their scope, depth, length, etc.) will be the requirements for publication in the *Journal of Communication*. No final dissertation (or final oral) will be required of the student. The point here is to have the student doing research at every stage of his work, not merely at the end. (At least one other point is that the student will be trained to do realistic and publishable research.) Moreover, by conducting three studies, students will gain experience in using different methods of discovering knowledge. The "team" effort would in all cases be the first study. The team would be headed by a professor who would provide "on-the-job" research training for the inexperienced student. The later studies would be conducted by the student alone.

The area of communications or media research is very wide indeed, and has many parts almost completely uncharted. For example (as McLuhan has pointed out), until a few years ago, one could not find a single paragraph written about the effects of the printed page on human perception. Some other questions that are relatively untouched are these: What specific effects are television, film, LP record, transistor radio, and the like, having on youth? To what extent are such media environments responsible for the "generation gap"? for student rebellion? for the search for "self" through drugs? What kinds of revolutions, if any, does electric circuitry provoke? Are books obsolete? If so, when will we find out? If not, what useful purposes will they serve? Why, indeed, can't Johnny read? Will he ever? Why should he? What are the long-range effects of the information explosion? Is it destroying hierarchies? organized religion? the industrial state? Who is programming the computers? What should computers be used for? What will they use us for? Who should be forbidden to use them? Are schools obsolete? What uses should be made of bugging devices? of the television-telephone? What is technology doing to the concept of "privacy"? What is the pill doing to our concepts of sex and marriage? of children? of religion? Will the electric car save our cities? At what cost? Are cities obsolete? Have big media "repealed" the Bill of Rights? Have they made politics an offshoot of show business? If so, what can we do about it? What new kinds of politics will we require? What will be our new literary forms? Of what use will "tradition" be? To what extent is technology remaking our language? Have the big media "polluted" our language environment? To what extent is our language impeding our understanding of technology?

This is not the place to discuss in detail the enormous possibilities for media research. However, three points need to be stressed about such research in the context of our program. First, the traditional categories of research (experimental, descriptive, etc.) will need to be expanded to include types of studies not conventionally valued—for example, speculative research. Second, and related, our students hopefully will pioneer in inventing new methods of discovering knowledge and gaining insight, since media research is not always useful when modeled after research in the physical sciences. And finally, we expect that great stress will be put on studies in the popular arts—that is, on the history, structure, and effects of the products of the mass media.

MEDIA PERSPECTIVES AND CRITICISM

Perhaps the most singular feature of the program will be the students' continuous participation in media criticism. This means that the students will produce, write, direct, edit, broadcast, tele-cast, etc., regular commentary about media of communication. The students will, in effect, monitor our media environment, addressing themselves to the national community. It is essential to note that there is no individual or institution presently engaged in such far-ranging criticism as we here have in mind.

The students will produce a bi-weekly television program (taped in our own studio), a weekly radio program (taped in our own studio), and a weekly newsletter, possibly even a monthly magazine. Their object will be to initiate and sustain a serious, informed dialogue with the national community on the interaction between human beings and their communications technology. The departure point is media as environments (media ecology)—that is, the effects of the structure and content of media on human perceptions, values, and understanding. Of paramount concern is the language environment itself—the uses and misuses of language, especially via the mass media. Our plans require that we reach out as far as possible into the community, so that many different kinds of citizens will look to our students for the most penetrating evaluations of our technological society. Our plans call for the following:

1. Review of the press—for which our students might take as their models the work of A. J. Liebling or Nat Hentoff. They would address themselves to such immediate and long-range questions as, How have newspapers dealt with important stories

of the week? How do newspapers decide what is an "important" story? What are the biases of different newspapers? What are their strengths? Who are the most reliable reporters? And so on. An adjunct activity will be correspondence with individual news reporters and editors. Each student will correspond regularly with one news reporter, including radio and TV men, on the quality of his work during a specified period of time.

2. Criticism of print and electronic advertising, in which the agencies producing various advertisements will be regularly examined and evaluated, along with the aesthetic and social value of their work.

3. Criticism of radio and television programs, in which, among other things, "ordinary" people are given the opportunity to express their opinions about network programming. One special feature might be the Weekly Murder Index, wherein an account is kept of the number and types of murders (and other brutalities) depicted weekly on network TV. Of a more positive nature, the criticism will attempt to make explicit the standards that might fairly be used to evaluate television and radio programs.

4. Monitoring the Language Pollution Index—wherein students keep track of the important public utterances of the week, with a view toward calling attention to the best, and especially the worst (that is, deceptive, illogical, oversimplified, vague, contradictory, etc.), use of language by public figures. With the increased outpouring of language through the mass media, it is essential that some check be made on the quality and direction of our semantic environment.

5. Description and analysis of the economic facts of the communications industry—by which the public will be informed of the financial structure of various media of communication. A major purpose of this activity will be to bring to the attention of the public, and to attempt to answer, such questions as, What financial interests are at stake in cable television, pay TV, and ETV? Why do magazines go out of business? What is the present and future role of unions in newspapers? What are the foreseeable effects of automation on publishing?

Other student activities within the area of Media Perspectives and Criticism would include:

Informing the public about relevant government hearings and legislation dealing with media and technology;

Evaluating textbooks and the products of educational publishers;

Informing the public about the substance of major professional conferences and meetings dealing with media and technology;

and, most important,

Informing the public about new technologies and the effects they are likely to have on the structure of society. Here is an invaluable contribution, since there is at present virtually no public dialogue on the proliferation of new technologies nor of their possibilities for good or ill.

The purposes of the students' activities in Media Perspectives and Criticism are these:

1. Our students will learn how to conduct responsible media criticism and will become, hopefully, the nucleus of a cadre of media critics absolutely needed if our society is to deal rationally with present and future problems.

2. Our students will develop models of and standards for media criticism, where very few presently exist.

3. Our program will serve the community by becoming a major resource and focus for discussions of the impact of communications technology on society.

Two more features of this area of activity must be mentioned. First, seminars will be conducted when needed in order to assist students in their efforts. These seminars will be conducted by specially invited practitioners of the communication arts—for example, Peter Brook, Stanley Kubrick, Mike Nichols, Russell Baker, Gay Talese, Burt Lancaster, John Lennon, Frank Stanton, et al. Second, we will arrange for each of our students to "intern" (probably for a period of several weeks) with at least two different practitioners. The student will function as an "assistant," or in whatever capacity that will offer him the best opportunity to observe the inner workings of a medium of communication. The purpose here is to give the student a direct sense of what the media look like from the inside. Our students will intern with film directors, book publishers, newspaper and magazine editors, television, radio, and record producers, advertising executives, and people similarly engaged in the communications industry.

The entire program is envisioned as of three years' duration, at the end of which time a Ph.D. would be awarded.

"Celibacy does not suit a university. It must mate itself with action."

ALFRED NORTH WHITEHEAD

LIMITS

The Greeks had a word for it. *Hubris.* Going beyond the limits, and suffering the consequences.

It is, for most of us, an unhappy fact of life that there are limits to everything. We are just beginning to learn the limits of technological "progress." The hard way.

It isn't easy to know what the limits are, but we dare not ignore the fact that they are there, in everything, always.

Bertrand Russell who, whatever he was, was certainly not a part of *any* establishment, got off some characteristically incisive observations shortly before his death. They included the following:

> I think freedom is not a panacea. In the relationship between nations there ought to be less freedom than there is. To some degree this applies to modern education too. Both in education and in other matters, I think that freedom must have very definite limitations, where you come to things that are definitely harmful to other people, or things that prevent you yourself from being useful, such as lack of knowledge.

Breaking Bread

There is something about human beings sharing basic survival activities, like making love, fighting a common threat, and eating, that brings them closer together—emotionally as well as physically —than they would ever get otherwise.

One of the best ways for communication to occur is through the communion-like process of sharing food. Think about it. Sharing food with someone provides the opportunity for a kind of communication—though it is by no means automatic—that is rare. If the opportunity is fruitful and the communication develops, a sense of community of interests and concerns begins to grow.

All this is by way of posing a situation for you: In most schools (secondary or college), it is common for the faculty to have separate (if not private, or equal) eating facilities. It seems to us that this compounds the communication problem that the usual classroom procedures produce: confining teacher-student talk to questions about "the subject matter." The opportunity for students and faculty to use the space-time available for communion-communication during food-sharing seems to us to be worth working for. We know it isn't very dramatic, but we believe it is the kind of change that not only complements the sense of the soft revolution, but can be most effective in a number of indirect and unobtrusive ways that you can name as well as we.

So, just for the exercise, assume or pretend (if you have to) that you want to change the eating arrangements at your school so that faculty and students can eat together. See what kinds of strategies you can invent that are most likely to have the effect of accomplishing this little change in your school environment.

THE FIRST LAW of ERTIA:
Get It Together.
Organize.

There is no sense in "knowing" something if you don't act as if you know it. It's old, and everybody "knows" that "in unity there is strength," but most people "don't want to get involved" or are "too busy" to get together to *do* something that needs doing in an organized way. So somebody—like you—has to act as if he knows that power can be generated through organized action.

One of the most common student complaints we hear is that students are "powerless." This is not the result of any conspiracy to keep students from having power. It is the result of students' not doing anything to mobilize their potential power so that it becomes operational. The probability of *any* system's thrusting power upon someone who wants to change it is so remote as to be nonexistent. The general lack of student power is more a result of student apathy and inertia than anything else.

At the college where one of us works, for example, a general referendum was held on the adoption of a report of recommendations to change the process of campus governance. The recommendations called for a markedly higher degree of student participation in policy formation, virtually to the point where students enjoyed parity with faculty and administration in such matters. Despite the fact that the polls were open at least eight hours a day for five consecutive days, *only 11 per cent* of the student body was recorded as having voted, and the number of repeat votes in this percentage can only be guessed at.

The point is that if you are serious about generating student power, the biggest difficulty you face is that of organizing—unionizing, perhaps—your fellow students so that you can take positions and then speak and act *together*. Such an organization would become a power in school affairs simply because it exists.

Whatever human beings accomplish in the way of solving problems is the result of cooperation. That's just the way it is. Try to think of an exception.

Cooperation depends upon organization.
Organization depends upon agreement.
Agreement depends upon effective communication.
And all three depend on each other.
Try to effect one all by itself without the others.
Or try any two without the other one.
And see what happens.

Any time you have "a failure to communicate," you are making like Cool Hand Luke, and that means a wipeout.

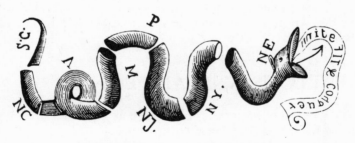

JOIN or DIE

Students Are People

The idea that students in public schools have "rights" is foreign to some school administrators. Yet the Supreme Court in recent years has clearly said that "rights" don't end at the school gates, and that people may not be deprived of their rights just because they are under twenty-one. It is also true that courts have been concerned with maintaining discipline in schools, and things that disrupt normal school activities may be stopped. State laws also make school boards and other officials responsible for what happens in the schools. But the Constitution is the highest law in the land, and rights won't be won unless they're tested. Knowing the rules at your school, especially if they are in writing, is the first step. Here are a few other things to keep in mind, all of which have been summarized for your use by Mr. Steven Nagler, who, as of this writing, is Director of the New Jersey Chapter of the American Civil Liberties Union.

BUTTONS AND ARMBANDS

The wearing of personal symbols such as armbands or buttons is protected by the First Amendment.

LEAFLETS

Schools also may not make rules that forbid the distribution of literature, or literature that is controversial. Many schools try to do this by requiring you to get approval before distributing leaflets and then refusing to permit anything on a controversial subject to be handed out.

The ACLU believes that any kind of a "prior-censorship" rule is unconstitutional, and that schools have no right to approve or disapprove in advance the content of literature you want to distribute; but the law isn't settled yet, and in many schools you may risk suspension if you distribute leaflets without prior approval. It's a good idea to get legal advice, if your school has that kind of rule. Schools may to some extent regulate the time and place of leaflet distribution on school grounds, and may stop the distribution of business literature or leaflets which urge students to break the law. Leaflets which use so-called "obscene" language, urge students to miss classes or otherwise undermine school authority, are likely to provoke a strong reaction. The safest thing to do is get legal advice in advance, if you have reasons to expect a problem.

Leafletting off school grounds, and not during school hours, should not be regulated by school officials. As a general rule, the closer you come to the classroom, and class time, the more regulation school officials impose.

FORMING ORGANIZATIONS, MEETINGS IN SCHOOLS

Schools usually require groups to have faculty advisers before they will recognize them. If you can't get a faculty adviser to "volunteer", this should not be an excuse for preventing you from meeting or forming a group. If any clubs are given scheduled meeting times and places, all clubs should receive the same privileges. State laws usually make exceptions as to social fraternities and sororities. The same rule of thumb applies to meetings as to leafletting: The closer you come to the classroom and class time, the more regulation you can expect. This is also true of picketing or demonstrations.

SEARCHES

Unless an emergency situation (such as a bomb threat) exists, the ACLU believes that school officials may not search students' lockers or other property without a search warrant from a court. The law is not settled on this point yet, and you should seek legal advice if this is a problem at your school. Many schools make students sign a letter giving permission to search before they give you a locker. Even if you sign such a paper, it probably won't affect your legal rights.

INQUISITIONS

Where a crime is being investigated, a suspect has a right to refuse to answer questions and to have a lawyer present. This applies to students in schools just as it does to other people. It doesn't matter whether the questioning is done by the police or a school official. The school should at least notify your parents before they try to question you about a crime.

SUSPENSIONS and EXPULSIONS

The ACLU believes that students have a right to a hearing, notice of charges, and legal help at the hearing before a suspension or expulsion. The law is clear about the right to a hearing where long suspensions or expulsions are involved, but not where a student is suspended for only a few days. If an emergency exists the courts usually permit suspensions before hearings. If possible, legal advice should be sought even before disciplinary action is taken.

PARADING AND STREET SPEECHES

Where traffic may be obstructed or actual violence is imminent, police can properly intervene. If violence is threatened against you, the police are supposed to protect you, not stop you. Where some traffic obstruction may occur such as where tables are being set up, or a parade is planned, letting the police know in advance may avoid problems. Parades or similar activities which may block traffic sometimes require permits. The same is true when sound equipment is involved.

Permit laws that require weeks of advance notice, fingerprinting, large fees or lists of all participants are probably invalid and you should seek legal help. Permits may not be denied without good reason, or denied to one group if they are granted to any other group at different times. Parade permits allow you to obstruct traffic, while spelling out the time, place, and extent of the parade.

MEETING IN PUBLIC BUILDINGS

Meeting rooms in public buildings or other public places, should be available to all groups if they are available to any group. If weeks of notice are required or local officials refuse to rent facilities or make unusual requirements, get legal help.

FUND RAISING

If you are selling newspapers or asking for contributions on the street or door to door, some towns may require you to get a permit. Peddling-license requirements do not apply. What has been said before about parade permits applies here too.

LOITERING AND OTHER FORMS OF HARASSMENT

A wide variety of loitering, curfew and other similar laws are commonly used to harass people who look different or express unpopular views. Such laws are frequently unconstitutional and you should seek legal help if you have a problem.

THE GENERATION GAP

It's hard to get legal help if parents won't back up the student, but the situation may not be hopeless, particularly if someone else over twenty-one is willing to help.

PRIVATE SCHOOLS

Much of what is said above doesn't apply to private schools, although it should. Yet, even private schools in some cases may be compelled by legal action to treat students fairly.

Below is a statement of the joint recommendations of the ACLU and the American Association of University Professors concerning student freedoms:

Twelve Freedoms for Students

Recommendations of the ACLU and the AAUP

1) *Freedom of expression.* Students and student organizations: "should be free to discuss, pass resolutions, distribute leaflets, circulate petitions, and take other lawful action respecting any matter which directly or indirectly concerns or affects them." (ACLU) They "should be free to examine and to discuss all questions of interest to them, and to express opinions publicly or privately." (AAUP)

2) *Freedom of the press.* "All student publications—college newspapers, literary and humor magazines, academic periodicals and yearbooks—should enjoy full freedom of the press." Any board supervising student publications "should be composed of at least a majority of students. . . . neither a faculty member nor an administrator should exercise veto power over what should be printed." (ACLU) "The student press should be free of censor-

ship and advance approval of copy, and its editors and managers should be free to develop their own editorial policies and news coverage." (AAUP)

3) *Freedom of association.* "Students should be free to organize and join associations for educational, political, social, religious or cultural purposes. . . . affiliation with any extramural association . . . , so long as it is an open affiliation, should not of itself bar a group from recognition." (ACLU) "Students should be free to organize and join associations to promote their common interests. . . . Affiliation with an extramural organization should not of itself affect recognition of a student organization." (AAUP)

4) *Freedom to choose speakers and topics.* "Students should be accorded the right to assemble, to select speakers and to discuss issues of their choice. . . . Permission should not be withheld because the speaker is a controversial figure." (ACLU) "Students should be allowed to invite and to hear any person of their own choosing. While the orderly scheduling of facilities may require the observance of routine procedures before a guest speaker is invited to appear on campus, institutional control of campus facilities should never be used as a device of censorship." (AAUP)

5) *Freedom to protest.* "Student organizations and individual students should be allowed, and no special permission should be required, to distribute pamphlets, except in classrooms and study halls, or collect names for petitions concerning either campus or off-campus issues. Orderly demonstrations on campus should not be prohibited." (ACLU) Students should "be free to support causes by any orderly means which do not disrupt the regular and essential operation of the institution." (AAUP)

6) *Freedom from discrimination.* "Just as the college should not discriminate on grounds of race, religion, color or national origin in its admission policies, so should it not permit discrimination in any area of student life, such as housing on or off the campus, athletics, fraternities, social clubs." (ACLU) "While sectarian institutions may give admission preference to students of their own persuasion, such a preference should be clearly and publicly stated. College facilities and services should be open to all students, and institutions should use their influence to secure equal access for all students to public facilities in the local community." (AAUP)

[157]

7) Freedom from disciplinary action without due process. "No student should be expelled or suffer major disciplinary action for any offense, other than failure to meet the required academic standards, without having been advised explicitly of the charges against him, which at his request should be in writing. He should be free to seek the counsel . . . of his choice. . . . he may ask for a hearing . . . by a faculty-student [or] faculty committee. . . . [he] should be allowed to call witnesses . . . and cross-examine those who appear against him. . . . a final appeal to the board of trustees should be allowed." (ACLU) "In developing responsible student conduct, disciplinary proceedings play a role substantially secondary to counseling, guidance, admonition, and example. In the exceptional circumstances when these preferred means fail to resolve problems of student conduct, proper procedural safeguards should be observed to protect the student from the unfair imposition of serious penalties," and should include, among many features, a hearing in which "the burden of proof should rest upon the officials bringing the charge." (AAUP)

8) Freedom from arbitrary regulation of conduct. "Regulations governing the conduct of students should be enacted by a committee composed of students, administrators, and faculty members if desired." (ACLU) "The student body should have clearly defined means to participate in the formulation and application of regulations affecting student affairs." (AAUP)

9) Freedom to use rights as a private citizen. "In their non-academic life, private or public, students should be free from college control. On the other hand, the college should not be held responsible for the nonacademic activities of its individual students." (ACLU) "As citizens, students should enjoy the same freedom of speech, peaceful assembly, and right of petition that other citizens enjoy. Faculty members and administrative officials should insure that institutional powers are not employed to inhibit . . . their off-campus activities and their exercise of the rights of citizenship." (AAUP)

10) Freedom from improper disclosure. "When interrogated directly or indirectly by prospective employers of any kind . . . , a teacher can safely answer questions which he finds clearly concerned with the student's competence and fitness for the job. . . . But, questions relating to the student's loyalty and patriotism, his political or religious or moral or social beliefs and attitudes, his general outlook, his private life, may if answered jeopardize the teacher-student relation." (ACLU) "Information about student views, beliefs, and political associations which professors acquire in the course of their work as instructors, advisers, and counselors should be considered confidential. Protection against improper disclosure is a serious professional obligation." (AAUP)

11) Freedom from off-campus denial of rights. "When students run into police difficulties off the campus in connection with what they regard as their political rights—as, for example, taking part in sit-ins, picket lines, demonstrations, riding on freedom buses—the college authorities should take every practical step to assure themselves that such students are protected in their full legal rights . . . [such as] fair trials in a court of law . . . speedy trials . . . that they are not abused by the police . . . that bail be sought and furnished . . . that appeals be taken when necessary." (ACLU) "Activities of students may upon occasion result in violation of law. In such cases, institutional officials should apprise students of their legal rights and may offer other assistance." (AAUP)

12) Freedom of thought in the classroom. "Students are responsible for learning thoroughly the content of any course of study, but they should be free to take reasoned exception to the data or views offered, and to reserve judgment about matters of opinion. . . . Students are responsible for maintaining standards of academic performance established by their professors, but they should have protection through orderly procedures against prejudiced or capricious academic evaluation." (AAUP)

Ten Smart Things
You Can Do Anytime
in the Next Two Weeks

1. Subscribe to one of the listener-sponsored radio stations that are part of the Pacifica Foundation. In the New York area, the station is WBAI; in Los Angeles, KPFK; in San Francisco, KPFA; and in Houston, KPFT. These stations are important avenues for the communication of dissenting ideas. They also give vivid expression to the life-style and opinions of young people. In fact, if you could get together a tape that would be worth hearing, it will almost certainly be given respectful attention by the staffs at these stations. In other words, these are media you can use, instead of their using you. And yet the stations are always in financial trouble. Apparently the inhabitants of the counter-culture don't like to put their money where their mouths are. Try it. Your subscription is tax-deductible, and there are special rates for students.

2. Familiarize yourself with the local representative of the American Civil Liberties Union; that is, find out who he is, talk with him, and learn something about the various cases his chapter is working on. The ACLU has been particularly interested in students' rights cases, and has sponsored conferences on the subject. Find out about them. Maybe even get involved in planning one.

3. If you want to work with Nader's Raiders, write to:

> The Center for the Study of Responsive Law
> 1908 Q Street N.W.
> Washington, D.C. 20009

4. Last year, John Gardner, former Secretary of Health, Education, and Welfare (he resigned from Johnson's cabinet), and organizer of the "Third Force" in American politics, said to the startled regulars on the *Today* show on NBC that "We need to shake up and renew our institutions, and the system they comprise" in order to make them more responsive to the real survival problems we face. He also said that working within the existing political parties would be fruitless. His purpose in organizing the "Third Force" is a product of his belief that "The national mood of anxiety and discouragement can be altered not by rhetoric but by specifying constructive goals and showing people a means of working toward those goals."

He said that anyone interested in working in this direction could get more information by writing to:

Common Cause
2100 M Street, N.W.
Washington, D.C. 20037
or phone: (202) 2931530

5. Subscribe to these magazines:

This Magazine Is About Schools
56 Esplanade Street East
Suite 301
Toronto 215, Ontario, Canada

Social Policy
P.O. Box 534
Cooper Station
New York, New York 10003

Outside the Net
P.O. Box 184
Lansing, Michigan 48901

They will give you access to some of the best ideas in the radical school movement.

6. If you have some instructive story to tell about how you or some others made a positive change in a school situation, write a note about it to Nat Hentoff at *The Village Voice* in New York

City. If he agrees that it is instructive, he will probably print your letter. Ditto for us, since N.P., as of this writing, has a regular radio program on WBAI in New York. It's called *Education Commentary*.

7. Subscribe to the

> New Schools Exchange Newsletter
> 301 East Canon Perdido
> Santa Barbara, California

The newsletter will keep you informed of developments in the "free school" movement, and will also print your letter if you are completely fed up with your present school and are looking for an alternative. They will also send you a useful directory of experimental schools.

8. You can also get help in this direction by writing to Len Solo or Stan Barondes at

> The Teacher Dropout Center
> Box 521
> Amherst, Massachusetts

This is a clearinghouse of information on innovative, community, and alternative schools. Its main function is to assist teachers in finding jobs in such schools, but it can also be of great help to students, especially if you just can't cut it any longer in your present situation.

9. Read Herbert Kohl's *The Open Classroom* and George Dennison's *The Lives of Children*. Get your parents to read them, and, if you can, your teachers. If you are an "education" major in college, ask your professors what they think.

10. And speaking of parents, teachers, and professors, why don't you pick one of them and write him or her a letter? Private letters are, sadly, a dying form of communication. But maybe for that very reason they have a curious power to command attention. Write down what's bugging you and why. It'll help you, and maybe them.

TEACHER POWER

𝍷𝍷 𝍷𝍷 𝍷𝍷 𝍷𝍷 𝍷𝍷

The U.S. Census Bureau reported early in 1970 that the median age of Americans is 27.7. That means that half the population is older than that, and, of course, that half is younger. And what *that* means is in the process of being worked out. But here's something that will help you to think about it:

As of July 1970, a survey by the New York State Education Department showed that almost half (49 per cent) of the teachers in the state were under thirty-two years of age. Only one-fifth were between forty-nine and sixty-four. This means that, so far as age is concerned, the gap between students and teachers is closing. And *that* means that there is a greater likelihood than ever that the perceptions and interests of students will be shared by their teachers. Up to now, teachers have been in an adversary relationship with students, to a great extent because they represented the interests of an older culture. We are now on the verge of a situation where *almost everybody in school—students* and *teachers—will be of the post-TV generation.* This is dynamite. But unless handled properly, it will blow up our best chances for significant change. Bear in mind:

that teachers are still public employees, who are hired by older, more conservative people—and can be fired by them;

that teachers, even the youngest ones, usually have more at stake in the existing system than do students;

and that teachers, no matter what their age, still are apt to be more conservative than students in their life-styles.

[163]

In short, students and teachers ought to be able to get together, but not *entirely* on the students' terms. For example, one of the suggestions made to teachers in *The Guerrilla Manual*, mentioned elsewhere in this handbook, is to begin a job interview by shouting, "I don't take shit from anybody!" If the education revolution is to depend on such moves as that, we can forget about the whole thing right now. In the first place, there aren't many teachers—even in the twenty-one to twenty-five age range—who would do that. And in the second place, those who would just wouldn't get jobs.

Here's a story of how some things *did* get changed by young faculty members. A group of junior high school teachers, all under thirty, came to the conclusion that the curriculum laid out by their department chairman (an older person, as it happened) was not justified by anything other than "tradition." They wanted to change it into something else that would be more responsive to the interests and needs of their students and of their community. After generating a great deal of hostility by challenging the authority of the department head (who had the support of the principal), the young teachers reassessed the situation and began to try a judo approach: using the existing values of the system against itself.

Recognizing that the forms of authority they had to deal with in the school responded to other forms of authority outside the school, the young teachers acquired the services of a sympathetic university professor as a "consultant" to help them with "curriculum development." The central administration, the superintendent, and the principal viewed having a professor from a prestigious university working in the school as a very desirable public relations device; and administrators are always looking for good public relations devices. The response, in brief, was strongly positive.

The professor met with the teachers, and with the administration (to get some perspective on the ingredients of the system). Being convinced of the desirability of what the teachers wanted to do, and understanding the sources of resistance, he worked out a strategy that involved a higher authority than either the department head or the central administration—because he knew that their values would lead them to defer to it.

The professor knew that the state education department had an agency whose function it was to help schools produce innovations in curriculum and teaching. (It can be helpful if someone involved in a change process is well-informed.) So he and the teachers prepared a proposal to submit to this agency, incorporating the changes the teachers wanted to make in a language the agency would accept, and submitted it. Not only did the agency approve the proposal, it provided funds to help the teachers pay for the supplies needed in the development of new curriculum materials.

Once this happened, the administration became an active source of support because of the opportunity to cooperate with the state education department. They were proud to have their school selected by the state "to be a leader in curriculum innovation."

The teachers, with the help of a professor who understood how the system worked, had found a soft spot in the system and used it to eliminate a boring and pointless traditional curriculum, and to get the opportunity to work on inventing a new, open-ended curriculum of their own.

The professor also managed to use the system against itself, since the materials developed by him and the teachers and their students were later published, thus adding to his "authority" in the system and increasing his power to effect similar changes in many other schools.

Not as flashy as saying "I won't take shit from anybody," but there are an awful lot of kids in that junior high school who are having a better time of it because these teachers were willing to use judo.

Now, the question is, What can *students* do to help teachers become productive agents of change? Here are six things worth trying at almost any level in the school hierarchy.

1. Help your teachers to become better informed. As a student, you have more time to read, see movies, listen to records, and so on, than your teachers, who very often are just "poor working stiffs" (professors included). We know of dozens of instances where students have turned teachers around by giving them a book or two to read. (Once it was even *Teaching as a Subversive*

Activity.) The best book as of this writing would probably be Charles Silberman's *Crisis in the Classroom,* which is a report of a three-year Carnegie Corporation study of schools. Silberman, his consultants, and the Carnegie Corporation are all establishment sources, and the book cannot be easily dismissed as the ravings of a malcontent.

You might also familiarize your teachers with relevant research on such matters as grading, homogeneous grouping, and teaching methods. This suggestion will strike you as unrealistic only if you and your fellow students are not organized. If you are organized, you can form a committee whose function it is to keep informed on the most significant research in education and to acquaint teachers with the findings. If the suggestion still seems unrealistic, try to remember what we said at the beginning of this handbook: The use of judo requires some heavy thinking. To this, let us add that it requires heavier thinking of those who want to change the system than of those who do not. Keep in mind something else we say in another part of the handbook: The basic tool we have for keeping entropy under control is information. What we are saying here is that students can be of tremendous help in making teachers act smart, *if* they assume the function of feeding information, rather than slogans, into the system.

Incidentally, if you are organized, you can also feed into the system information about alternative curricula and schools. You would be surprised at how many teachers do *not* know of the existence of the Parkway School in Philadelphia, or of Goddard College, or of Harlem Prep, or even of the alternative school "movement." Many teachers are not *against* these things; they just don't know about them.

2. Try to create new materials, including methods of evaluation for your teachers to use. There are not many teachers around who would refuse to use books, films, records, articles, cartoons, and especially questions brought to them by students. This is particularly true in the matter of evaluation. If students in a particular class—high school or college—were serious about proposing a method of evaluation different from the conventional one, a substantial number of teachers would go for it. In fact, teachers are usually *flattered* when students take such initiatives. It is assumed to be a sign of independence and creativity,

and teachers like to *say* that they are working toward these goals.

3. Invite teachers to student meetings, rallies, and even bull sessions. In the first place, you would be astonished to know how many teachers agree with student complaints but stay away from the struggle because they can find no way to ally themselves with students. In the second place, there are very few teachers anywhere who are not flattered by an invitation to join with or speak to student groups. This is true even of teachers who do not agree with what students are saying. In the third place, there are many teachers who know their way around the system and would be delighted to give you judo lessons. In the fourth place—and this is the most judoish reason of all—if you ask someone who disagrees with you to address you or join with your group, how can he continue to disagree with you in quite the same way?

4. In talking to teachers, avoid saying dumb things like "If you're not with us, you're against us."

5. If you are turning on with drugs, don't make it awkward for your teacher-allies by advertising it. It is one thing for a *student* to say he's on drugs; it is quite another for a teacher to become implicated. The fastest way for a teacher to get fired these days is for it to become common rumor that he "encourages" drug use among students, even if that "encouragement" only takes the form of "accepting" what you do on your own time and outside of school. In other words, if you are dumb enough to be "in to" drugs, confine the damage to yourself. And incidentally, beware of teachers who commonly use such expressions as "turn on," "in to," "grass," and the like. They may be pandering to your prejudices, and might not be your friends.

6. Suggest new courses. There are many good teachers who simply cannot function outside the framework of a "course." They are in favor of change, but not if it would eliminate the security blanket that a course provides. At the same time, these teachers are interested in film, TV, rock music, ecology, photography, and other interests of young people. If you could invent courses on these subjects, you might find a great deal of support from the faculty.

Finally, remember that the teaching profession comes out of a tradition of subservience. Teachers have always been more or less a servant class, and even in an age of increased teacher militancy (that is, the growth of teacher unions), you cannot expect them to *lead* any movements for change. But they will follow if a context is provided that permits them to function according to their own temperament and style.

Getting It Together
Also Means
Keeping It Together

Since change is *the* fact of our times, why not suggest that a "course" be offered for credit every quarter or semester, in which students, faculty, and administration would continuously monitor the school as a system and feed into the policy-making process informed recommendations for change that grow out of the course. This would be one way of continuously renewing the school as changing circumstances require.

It's Hardly Worth Saying, But...

Never assume that *anybody* you have to deal with knows what he's doing, much less why.

Keep asking questions—of yourself, as well as of those who are working with you and of those you are working on.

Follow up every step of every strategy you work out.

If everything isn't followed up, expect everything to get fouled up.

**That (*however "cynical" it may sound*)
is just the way it is.**

Shh...
Some Soft
Revolutionaries
at Work

Stephen Kass and Philip Kosdan, as of this writing, are under-graduate students at NYU. They were not altogether happy with the administration's proposal for an Urban Studies program. They submitted their own. After months of negotiation and back-door politicking, they succeeded in initiating an eight-point course (of which they are presently the administrators). As of right now, twenty-two undergraduates are enrolled in the course. Below is the syllabus.

TO ALL STUDENTS AT NEW YORK UNIVERSITY: AN-NOUNCING A NEW COURSE IN METROPOLITAN STUDIES. DOUBLE COURSE.

W 99.0250—INTERNSHIP

THIS COURSE WILL INVOLVE WORKING IN AN OR-GANIZATION OR AGENCY DEALING IN URBAN PROBLEMS FOR TWO FULL DAYS A WEEK. THE PURPOSE OF THE INTERNSHIP COURSE IS TO GIVE STUDENTS FIRST-HAND KNOWLEDGE NOT SIMPLY OF URBAN PROBLEMS

BUT, MORE IMPORTANT, OF ATTEMPTS AT THEIR SOLU-
TION. ALTHOUGH SEVERAL OF THE PARTICIPATING
AGENCIES REQUIRE INTENSIVE RESEARCH INTO AN
URBAN PROBLEM AREA, ALL OF THE AGENCIES ARE
COMMITTED TO ACTION, SOLUTIONS AND SOCIAL
CHANGE.

THE FOLLOWING WILL INCLUDE A LIST OF SOME
OF THE AGENCIES AND BRIEF DESCRIPTIONS OF EACH
AGENCY AND THE POSITIONS AND ROLES THAT WILL
BE PLAYED BY THE STUDENT:

1. ENVIRONMENT!—ENVIRONMENT! IS ATTEMPTING TO
COORDINATE THE ACTIVITIES OF ALL EAST COAST
GROUPS WORKING ON "CREEPING ENVIRONMENTAL AN-
NIHILATION" AND CONDUCTING ITS OWN RESEARCH
AND ACTION PROGRAMS. RESEARCH IS USUALLY
MUCKRAKING. WHO IS RESPONSIBLE FOR POLLUTION IN
THIS AREA OF THE CITY? WHY ARE THERE NO PARKS
IN THIS AREA AND WHO IS RESPONSIBLE? REAL ES-
TATE INTERESTS? ETC. ACTION CAN INCLUDE ANY-
THING FROM ORGANIZING A CITY-WIDE DEMONSTRATION
TO HELPING RESIDENTS IN THE CONSTRUCTION OF A
PEOPLE'S PARK. STUDENTS WILL CARVE OUT THEIR
OWN ROLE IN THIS ORGANIZATION.

2. TEAM—THE EDUCATION ACTION MOVEMENT BUILDS
COMMUNITY EDUCATION UNIONS, A DEMOCRATIC COALI-
TION OF PARENTS, STUDENTS AND SYMPATHETIC
TEACHERS IN LOCAL SCHOOLS. MEMBERS OF UNION LO-
CALS WORK TOWARD AN EVALUATION OF THE EDUCA-
TIONAL SYSTEM, AND THEN ATTEMPT TO ORGANIZE
OTHERS INTO THE UNION IN ORDER TO CREATE A
POWER BASE TO CHALLENGE EXISTING EDUCATIONAL
PRACTICES. WITH THE CREATION OF MANY UNION LO-
CALS, THE POWER MONOPOLY OF THE BOARD OF EDUCA-
TION AND U.F.T. CAN THEN BE CHALLENGED. STUDENTS
WILL PARTICIPATE AS FULL MEMBERS OF THE ORGANI-
ZATION: ORGANIZING HIGH SCHOOL STUDENTS, DEVEL-
OPING PROGRAMS AND MATERIALS, AND HELPING TO

CONDUCT WORKSHOPS ON EDUCATION AND ALTERNATIVE
EDUCATIONAL POSSIBILITIES.

3. THE NEW YORK CIVIL LIBERTIES UNION—THE
N.Y.C.L.U. WILL BE CONDUCTING A LARGE CAMPAIGN
ON THE STUDENTS' RIGHTS ISSUE. STUDENTS WILL
ACQUIRE LAY-LEGAL EXPERTISE IN STUDENTS' RIGHTS
AND PARENTS' RIGHTS AND ACT AS ADVISORS TO
GROUPS AND INDIVIDUALS. STUDENTS MAY ALSO BE
INVOLVED IN ORGANIZING STUDENTS AND PARENTS ON
A CITY-WIDE BASIS ON THESE ISSUES.

4. HEALTH PAC—THE HEALTH POLICY ADVISORY CEN-
TER DOES RESEARCH AND SOME ORGANIZING IN HEALTH
PROBLEMS. THEIR EXTENSIVE AND IN-DEPTH RESEARCH
ASSIGNMENTS ARE DETERMINED BY A DESIRE TO BUILD
GRASSROOTS MOVEMENTS. THEY ARE CURRENTLY PRE-
PARING MATERIALS FOR ORGANIZING LOWER-MIDDLE-
CLASS HOSPITAL WORKERS—NURSES AND SOCIAL
WORKERS—AND LOWER-CLASS CONSUMERS. THIS RE-
SEARCH IS PRIMARILY A MUCKRAKING OPERATION AS
KNOWLEDGE OF POOR MEDICAL SERVICES BECOMES
KNOWN TO THOSE PEOPLE HURT BY THEM AND DAN-
GEROUS TO THE PEOPLE WHO ARE RESPONSIBLE FOR
SUCH PRACTICES. STUDENTS WILL BE INVOLVED IN
THE COMPLETE OPERATION OF THE ORGANIZATION, IN-
CLUDING HELPING TO PUT OUT A MONTHLY BULLETIN.

5. THE UNIVERSITY OF THE STREETS—"THE UNIVER-
SITY OF THE STREETS IS AN ALTERNATIVE EDUCA-
TIONAL ENVIRONMENT WHICH ALLOWS PERSONS WHOM
THE EXISTING SYSTEM HAS FAILED TO LEARN THROUGH
DIRECT INVOLVEMENT IN COMMUNITY EDUCATION AND
DEVELOPMENT. THE UNIVERSITY EVOLVES AS THE PAR-
TICIPANTS MAKE IT EVOLVE." SERVICING 300 FULL-
TIME AND 300 PART-TIME STUDENTS ON THE LOWER
EAST SIDE, THE UNIVERSITY IS A CONSTANTLY
CHANGING AND INNOVATING OPERATION GOVERNED AND

RUN BY ITS STAFF AND A JUNIOR COUNCIL, AN
ELECTED GROUP OF STUDENTS. MOST OF ITS STUDENTS
ARE SCHOOL DROP-OUTS WHO NEED EXTENSIVE TUTOR-
ING ON A ONE TO ONE BASIS IN MATHEMATICS AND
ENGLISH. N.Y.U. STUDENTS WORKING IN THE TUTOR-
ING PROGRAM WILL ALSO BE INVOLVED IN THE OPERA-
TION OF THE UNIVERSITY AND FURTHER DEVELOPING
THE OPERATION OF THE PREP SCHOOL OF WHICH THE
TUTORING PROGRAM IS ONE PART. STAFF IS ALSO
NEEDED FOR THEIR DAY CARE CENTER, MUSIC AND
THEATER PROGRAMS, BOTH IN OPERATION AND PLAN-
NING. STUDENTS WITH SPECIAL EXPERTISE IN FUND
RAISING AND PUBLIC RELATIONS ARE ALSO NEEDED TO
WORK ON THE ADMINISTRATIVE STAFF. THE "SHADOW
SYSTEM" OF THE UNIVERSITY REQUIRES THAT EACH
STAFF MEMBER TRAIN A STUDENT OF THE UNIVERSITY
TO TAKE OVER HIS POSITION. THE PURPOSE OF THE
UNIVERSITY IS TO TAP THE INNATE POTENTIAL OF
ITS STUDENTS AND TURN THEM INTO A RESOURCE FOR
THE COMMUNITY.

6. TEACHERS INC.—THE TEACHERS INCORPORATED RE-
CRUITS, TRAINS, AND SUPPORTS TEACHERS WORKING
WITH PARENTS AND COMMUNITY ORGANIZATIONS FOR
REFORM OF THE PUBLIC SCHOOLS. EMPHASIS IS
PLACED ON COMMUNITY CONTROL OF EDUCATION AND
INSTITUTIONS, NEW TECHNIQUES IN CURRICULUM,
CLASSROOM ORGANIZATION AND MANAGEMENT AND
TEACHING STYLE. THERE ARE PLACEMENTS FOR STU-
DENTS ON THE LOWER EAST SIDE AND UPPER WEST
SIDE. STUDENTS CAN PERFORM ONE OR MORE OF SEV-
ERAL FUNCTIONS: TEACHER SENSITIVITY TRAINING,
WORKSHOPS FOR PARENTS AND STUDENTS ON EDUCA-
TIONAL ISSUES, RESEARCH, DEVELOPMENT AND PRO-
GRAM PLANNING, AND CAMPUS RECRUITMENT AT
EDUCATION DEPARTMENT FOR TEACHERS INC. STUDENTS
WILL CARVE OUT THEIR OWN SPECIFIC ROLE IN THE
ORGANIZATION AND MAY EVEN CREATE THEIR OWN PRO-
GRAMS WHICH THEY WILL RUN.

[174]

7. <u>WOMEN'S</u> <u>CENTER</u>——THE WOMEN'S CENTER IS A CLEARING HOUSE FOR MANY RESEARCH AND ORGANIZING PROJECTS OF DIFFERENT DURATION. THERE ARE PLACEMENTS IN PROJECTS IN HOUSING, ABORTION, CHILD CARE, NEWSPAPER WRITING AND PUBLICITY, JOB DISCRIMINATION AND GENERAL HEALTH. ALL THE PROJECTS ARE INVOLVED IN DIFFERENT ASPECTS OF WOMEN'S LIBERATION. STUDENTS MUST FIRST CHOOSE AN AREA OF INTEREST AND WILL THEN BE ASSIGNED A PLACEMENT OR SERIES OF PLACEMENTS.

8. <u>VIETNAM</u> <u>VETERANS</u> <u>AGAINST</u> <u>THE</u> <u>WAR</u>——(FOR VET-ERANS ONLY) STUDENTS ARE NEEDED TO DEVELOP PEACE EDUCATION PROGRAMS IN COMMUNITIES AND RESEARCH MATERIALS, AS WELL AS RECRUIT OTHER VETERANS ON CAMPUS. THE PURPOSE OF THIS ORGANI-ZATION IS TO DEVELOP A GRASSROOTS VETERANS' MOVEMENT AGAINST THE WAR IN VIETNAM.

9. <u>WELFARE</u> <u>RIGHTS</u> <u>ORGANIZATION</u>——THE WELFARE RIGHTS ORGANIZATION IS PART OF A NATIONAL OR-GANIZATION THAT HAS ORGANIZED WELFARE RECIPI-ENTS INTO A POWERFUL NATIONAL UNION. ALL THE STAFF DO ALL THE DIFFERENT KINDS OF WORK IN THE ORGANIZATION: RESEARCH (CURRENTLY INTO THE IN-ADEQUACIES OF THE FOOD STAMP PROGRAM), ORGANIZ-ING (CURRENTLY SUPPORT ON COLLEGE CAMPUSES), PAPER WORK, AND ANSWERING THE TELEPHONE. STU-DENTS BECOME FULL MEMBERS OF THE GROUP AND ARE DIRECTLY INVOLVED IN DECISION MAKING. IF THEY CHOOSE, STUDENTS MAY BE ASSIGNED TO A LOCAL UNION AND ASSIST AS AN ORGANIZER.

10. <u>EDUCATIONAL</u> <u>DEVELOPMENT</u> <u>PROGRAM</u>——A SERVICE ORGANIZATION FOR STUDENTS ON THE LOWER EAST SIDE WITH PROBLEMS IN EDUCATION. TUTORS. ADMIN-ISTRATORS WHO WILL ACT AS LIAISON TO PUBLIC SCHOOLS AND COLLEGES, EMPLOYMENT COUNSELORS, AND PERFORM OTHER SERVICES TO THE STUDENTS:

FINDING LEGAL ASSISTANCE, ETC. TUTORS WILL ALSO
FUNCTION AS ADMINISTRATORS.

THE INTERNSHIPS WILL BE SUPPLEMENTED AT THE
UNIVERSITY BY A PROGRAM OF EVALUATION AND WORK-
SHOPS THE NATURE OF WHICH WILL BE DECIDED UPON
BY ALL THE STUDENTS IN THE PROGRAM. A PROGRAM
HAS BEEN RECOMMENDED WHICH WILL INCLUDE BI-
WEEKLY EVALUATION SESSIONS CONDUCTED WITH ALL
THE INTERNS AT ONE AGENCY BY THE ASSISTANTS TO
THE INTERNSHIP PROGRAM AND BI-WEEKLY WORKSHOP
SESSIONS CONDUCTED WITH ALL THE INTERNS BY
GUEST PARTICIPANTS. THE THEME FOR THESE WORK-
SHOPS WOULD BE THE ROLE OF THE UNIVERSITY IN
THE COMMUNITY AND THE ROLE OF THE COMMUNITY IN
THE UNIVERSITY.

> ALL STUDENTS WHO REGISTER FOR THE INTERN-
> SHIPS ARE ADVISED TO TAKE OR AUDIT THE
> COURSE IN COMMUNITY ORGANIZING GIVEN IN THE
> METROPOLITAN STUDIES PROGRAM.

When asked to comment, in the form of advice to others, on
what they did to achieve their course and their role in it, here is
what Kass and Kosdan said:

> "Our first step was an exercise in utopian projection. It was
> translating a general, philosophical orientation into a concrete
> program.
> "Don't negotiate in your mind what 'they' will accept or reject.
> Don't be afraid to follow out your idea of an ideal program, the
> best possible program, what, in fact, you want.
> "We were constructing our own learning situation. Motivate
> other students to do the same, and then compare notes.
> "The next step is to get over everyone's mental constipation in
> negotiations and follow-through. Be smart. Do everything: all
> details. You have taken over: You are your own administrator,
> secretary, teacher, and student. This will involve you in constant
> hassles and negotiations. If you cannot go East, go West; if up is
> blocked off, go under or through—keeping your program first in

mind, although you may lose parts of it for a time. Forget personality conflicts, ideological idiocies, and fear of authority. Work off of your own authority."

If you feel that communicating with these guys would help you in any way, write to them,

> c/o Metropolitan Studies Program
> New York University
> 19 University Place
> New York, New York 10003

Meanwhile, at Goddard College in Plainfield, Vermont, you can get a Master's Degree without taking any courses, and without being confined to Plainfield, Vermont. The Goddard Graduate Program exists wherever its students and teachers can do their best work in solving problems and acquiring skills. The Graduate Program is, so to speak, in the student's head. And naturally the student determines the projects he or she wants to work on. Here is a reproduction of the application form for Goddard's Graduate Program. It is easily the most unusual, economical, and sensible application form in the Western Hemisphere.

```
GODDARD COLLEGE    /    Plainfield, Vermont 05667

The Graduate Program

STUDENT APPLICATION FORM          Date:_____
What is your name?  _____
Address?  _____

          _____
                         (zip code, please)
Telephone?_____    Date of birth?_____

    If you require financial aid, let us know
    in a separate letter, which will be kept
    confidential if you want it to be.

    Get three people who know you well to write
    to us, indicating how they view you. This
```

will be kept in confidence, too, if you
wish.

If you have supplementary materials (articles, pictures, samples of your work, etc.),
please send them along.

Write no more than a page on each of the
following:
1) Tell us about yourself in the past.
2) What are you into now?
3) What would you want to do in the Goddard
   Graduate Program?
4) What people or kinds of people would you
   like to work with? Supply names if you
   wish.
5) What was your schooling like? (Please
   have transcripts of all college work sent
   to us.) Do you have a bachelor's degree?

Return the completed form and a ten-dollar application fee to:
           GRADUATE PROGRAM OFFICE
           Goddard College
           Plainfield, Vermont 05667
The deadline is now!   Thank you.

At Harvard's New College, which is an authorized curriculum
designed and taught by students, started in the spring of 1969,
the following courses were given:

The Ecstasy of Learning
Working Conditions at Harvard
Marshall McLuhan and the Rehabilitation of American Youth
Herbert Marcuse: Eros and Repression in Society
Underground Newspapers

Nairobi College is located (would you believe?) at 805 Runny-
mede Street in East Palo Alto, California. But it is a college

without walls. The community is its campus, and courses are conducted in churches, faculty homes, recreation centers, and social service agencies. Every full-time student is required to work in the community, and the Board of Trustees is composed of students, faculty, and community members.

According to Dr. James E. Russell, president of The College of the Potomac, there should be no required courses, no exams, no grades, and almost complete freedom for students to pursue independently whatever subjects interest them. He says that he is not concerned with courses being integrated. He is concerned with *students* being integrated.

The BEAM school (Burlington Ecumenical Action Ministry) is in Burlington, Vermont. The adults in the school are called "enablers," not teachers, and they are hired by the students. Everybody in the school plays a role in making decisions. The power in the BEAM school lies in the Open Meetings which occur on a weekly basis. Everyone who attends—enablers and students— has one vote. A BEAM student: "It is one thing to go to a school, and an entirely different thing to have been one of the people who developed that very same school."

Robert Theobald and Jean Scott have put together *Teg's 1994,* a participation book. It is mimeographed (to avoid the impression of finality), and requires the reader to work with the text; it even invites correspondence to improve it. *Teg's 1994* examines the developments which may occur between 1970 and 1994 *if* mankind takes steps to ensure its survival. The book is based on the learning experiences of a young girl, Teg, age twenty, who gets an Orwell Fellowship to discover the significance of developments over the past twenty-five years and the directions in which further change is required. If you want to participate in *Teg's 1994,* write to: Personalized Secretarial Service, 5045 North 12th Street, Phoenix, Arizona.

Ed Carpenter, with the help of his wife Ann, got Harlem Prep started four years ago. They both had fairly good jobs at the time, but their sense of outrage at what the conventional schooling process was doing to black kids in Harlem caused them to "get involved." Ed and Ann are members of the B'Hai religion, whose philosophy is one of respect for the integrity of each individual, and this includes *all* people, no matter what color or creed. The faculty of Harlem Prep has included nuns and atheists, hard revolutionaries and soft, black and white, and several other intriguing combinations. As of this writing, close to two hundred kids who would otherwise have found themselves on the streets, probably permanently, have been accepted to colleges. Kids *learn* at Harlem Prep. Maybe because at the Prep they are given a second chance. Maybe because they love Harlem Prep and the Carpenters. Maybe because they play a decisive role in how the school is run. No one is quite sure. But they do learn. If you want to know more about this extraordinary education adventure, write to Ed or Ann at Harlem Prep, 135th Street and Eighth Avenue, New York City.

And if you'd like to know about a "global high school," write to Ed Wilson, Box 414, Bronx, NY, USA. For almost twenty years, Ed has had a dream that education should concern itself with trying to understand war, prejudice, poverty, ignorance, and disease. His own experience with poverty includes living for three weeks eating only one five-cent candy bar a day (while he was studying at the University of Chicago). He has recently begun to see his dream come close to realization. He is now the president of the Institute of International Community Action, which will try to bring together youth from all over the world to study global themes and to learn how to solve problems from a perspective as large as the planet itself.

And speaking of planetary themes, do you know about WORLD GAME? As described by its inventor, R. Buckminster Fuller, WORLD GAME is a scientific means for discovering the expeditious ways of using the world's resources so "efficiently and omniconsiderately" that a higher standard of living than anything we have ever known can be achieved for all of humanity. It is based on the assumption that present-day technology now makes it possible to provide humanity with all of its material needs *if* technology is put to that use. Fuller contends that intelligent amateurs can discover within a few weeks of research how this can be done. If you would like to start a WORLD GAME group, write to Buckminster Fuller at the University of Southern Illinois in Carbondale, and materials will be sent to you.

The Talent Corps, which used to be called The Women's Talent Corps, is now the College for Human Services, located in New York City, with a charter to grant students a two-year junior college degree. The College was started in 1964 with the idea of training poor women for para-professional jobs. It is now one of the most interesting experiments in higher education anywhere in the country. Most of its students are still women, and all of its students are adults—between twenty-one and sixty. The curriculum includes three days of work at some social agency (e.g., a school or hospital) and two days of classes. The entire program is problem-centered and people-centered, and the college gets about ten times as many applications as it can handle. Audrey Cohen is the executive director. That she is an outstanding soft revolutionary is proven by the fact that in negotiations with the New York school system, she got the system to waive the high school diploma requirement for her graduates (The Talent Corps does not require a high school diploma for admission), who can now get jobs as teachers' assistants and teachers in the New York schools.

If you think we need new kinds of schools that are good for kids, and you'd like to help guys like George Dennison, Paul Goodman, Nat Hentoff, John Holt, and Jonathan Kozol get such schools started, send one dollar to:

New Nation Seed Fund
Box 4026
Philadelphia, Pennsylvania 19118

The money will be used ONLY to do things that are good for kids.

At the Education Exploration Center, 3104 16th Avenue South, Minneapolis 55407, is a great group of people doing just about everything there is to do to make schools better. If you want to get some idea of what they are into, send them a card and ask to get their newsletter.

HOW SWEET IT IS

On December 3, 1970, Deborah Jean Sweet provided the last example of a soft revolutionary gesture before the print for this book was locked up. Deborah was handed a Young Americans Medal by Richard Nixon for her part in organizing a fund-raising march to buy food for poverty-stricken children. In a very soft voice she said to him, "I can't believe in your sincerity in giving these awards for service until you get us out of the Vietnam war." Deborah later said that Nixon's remarks prior to handing out the medals—"a small minority of young Americans who have lost faith,"—upset her because "I saw him using me as a symbol" for satisfied youth. Deborah's parents thought her statement was great.

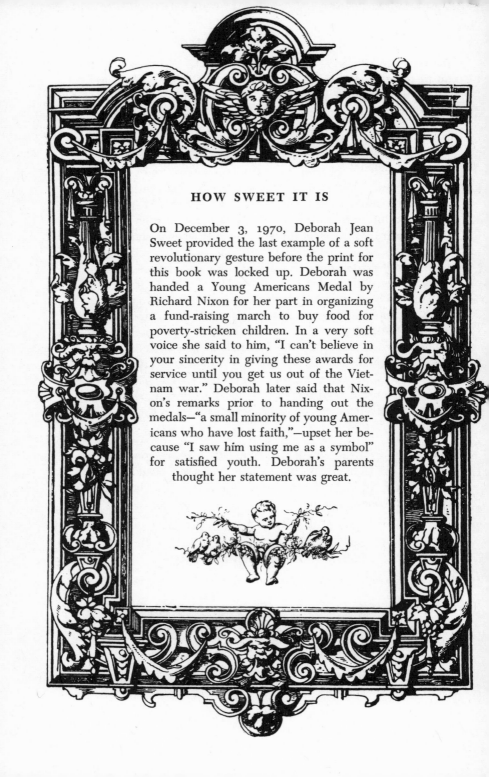